D0252717

Quinn

In Search of Excellence in Project Management

In Search of Excellence in Project Management

Successful Practices in
High Performance Organizations

Harold Kerzner

 VAN NOSTRAND REINHOLD
I(T)P® A Division of International Thomson Publishing Inc.

New York • Albany • Bonn • Boston • Detroit • London • Madrid • Melbourne
Mexico City • Paris • San Francisco • Singapore • Tokyo • Toronto

Copyright © 1998 by Van Nostrand Reinhold

I(T)P®   International Thomson Publishing Company.
          The ITP logo is a registered trademark used herein under license.

All rights reserved. No part of this work covered by the copyright hereon may be reproduced or used in any form or by any means—graphic, electronic, or mechanical, including photocopying, recording, taping, or information storage and retrieval systems—without the written permission of the publisher.

The ideas presented in this book are generic and strategic. Their specific application to a particular company must be the responsibility of the management of that company, based on management's understanding of their company's procedures, culture, resources, and competitive situation.

Printed in the United States of America.

http://www.vnr.com   Visit us on the Web!

For more information contact:

Van Nostrand Reinhold   Chapman & Hall GmbH
115 Fifth Avenue   Pappalallee 3
New York, NY 10003   69469 Weinham
USA   Germany

Chapman & Hall   International Thomson Publishing Asia
2-6 Boundary Row   60 Albert Street #15-01
London SEI 8HN   Albert Complex
United Kingdom   Singapore 189969

Thomas Nelson Australia   International Thomson Publishing Japan
102 Dodds Street   Hirakawa-cho Kyowa Building, 3F
South Melbourne 3205   2-2-1 Hirakawa-cho, Chiyoda-ku
Victoria, Australia   Tokyo 102 Japan

Nelson Canada   International Thomson Editores
1120 Birchmount Road   Seneca, 53
Scarborough, Ontario   Colonia Polanco
M1K 5G4, Canada   11560 Mexico D.F. Mexico

1 2 3 4 5 6 7 8 9 10 QEBFF 01 00 99 98 97

Library of Congress Cataloging-in-Publication Data

Kerzner, Harold.
    In search of excellence in project management : successful
practices in high performance organizations / Harold Kerzner.
        p.   cm.
    Includes index.
    ISBN 0-442-02706-0 (hardcover)
    1. Industrial project management. 2. Industrial management.
I. Title.
HD69.P75K468   1997
658.4'08–dc21   97-38003
                                            CIP

Production: Jo-Ann Campbell • mle design • 213 Cider Mill Road, Glastonbury, CT 06033

To my wife, Jo Ellyn,

who showed me that excellence can be achieved in
marriage, family, and life, as well as at work.

Acknowledgments

The author appreciates the staff members at the International Institute of Learning for their support in conducting the research for this book. In particular, the author is indebted to Jorge Calderon, who, once again, came to the author's rescue with quality graphics for presentations.

Contents

Preface

For over 30 years, we have done everything possible to prevent excellence in project management. We have provided lip service to empowerment, teamwork, and trust. We have hoarded information because information is power. We have placed functional decisions ahead of business decisions in the hierarchy of priorities. And we believed that time was a luxury rather than a constraint.

This mentality has disappeared thanks to the increased need to be competitive, to create quality products in a shorter period of time, and to develop trusting, long-term relationships with our clients. Businesses have changed for the better. Project failures are viewed as lessons learned (no more; who should we blame?). Trust and confidence between customers and contractors are at an all-time high. All of these factors have allowed corporations, regardless of their size, to reach for excellence in project management.

Words that were commonplace five years ago have taken on a new meaning today. Change is no longer viewed as being entirely bad. Today, change implies continuous improvement. Conflicts are no longer seen as detrimental. Conflicts managed well can be beneficial. Project management is no longer viewed as a system internal to the organization. It is now viewed as a competitive weapon that brings higher quality and value added to the customer. Companies that were considered excellent in management in the past may no longer be regarded as excellent today.

Consider the book entitled *In Search of Excellence,* written by Tom Peters and Robert Waterman in 1982. How many of those companies are still considered excellent today? How many of those companies have won the prestigious Malcolm Baldrige Award? How many of those companies are excellent in project management?

The changes that companies have undertaken in the past five years have been remarkable compared to the changes of the first 35 years of project management. This book discusses the changes that companies have made to achieve excellence in project management. Exact quotes have been provided by those who orchestrated the changes. The companies that are identified have either achieved some degree of excellence or are headed in the right direction to achieve excellence in the near future.

The Search for Excellence

Try to name one company, just one, that has given up on project management after implementing it. Probably you couldn't. Every company I know of that has adopted project management is still using it. Why? Because it works. Once a company has gone over to project management, the only question becomes: When will we achieve the full benefits of the system?

This chapter discusses the strategic imperatives driving the change to project management systems. A brief introduction to the basics of project management and the project management life cycle follow, with a briefing on the meaning of excellence in project management. Finally, the companies researched for this book are listed, along with my criteria for choosing to use them as examples of excellence.

Strategic Imperatives for Project Management

The strategic imperatives behind achieving excellence in project management come from two sources: internal and external. Internally, senior managers may discover the benefits of project management as they monitor general business trends in their industry or when they compare their company's results with those of its competitors. Internal champions of project management recognize potential overall improvements in both efficiency and effectiveness. They may also understand that project management can create future general managers versed in the operations of virtually every functional unit.

External pressures may force a company to accept the need for change in the way it does business. For example:

- Competition: Customers expect lower cost and the use of project management on their projects.
- Quality standards: Customers expect high quality, fewer failures, and fewer service calls.
- Financial outcomes: Customers expect contractors to accept lower profit margins.
- Legal concerns: Customers expect uniform project management systems that adhere to legal and regulatory boundaries (from the Environmental Protection Agency, for example).
- Technological factors: Customers expect state-of-the-art technology at reasonable prices.
- Social concerns: Employees want a system that allows them to do more work in less time in order to reduce the amount of overtime required.
- Political factors: Companies compete in a global economy that requires uniform project management processes.
- Economic pressures: Companies need to perform more work in less time and at a lower cost to reduce the impact of monetary exchange rates and the cost of borrowing money.
- Stockholders' concerns: Stockholders want internal growth and external expansion through mergers and acquisitions, which must be executed quickly and cost-effectively.

The benefits of project management have been demonstrated by numerous corporations. For example:

- Hewlett-Packard has shown increased sales and customer satisfaction.
- 3M has reduced its product development time from four to three years on average.
- Radian International has garnered more repeat business and happier clients; it has also reduced cost overruns and write-offs.
- Battelle (PNNL) has achieved better on-time and on-budget product delivery; it also has been offered noncompetitive contract extensions.
- OEC Medical Systems has reduced its average number of service calls, by 27 percent in the first 12 months of product life and 44 percent in the first 24 months.

Another strategic benefit of project management is that it can be integrated successfully with other management systems. The four most relevant today are concurrent engineering (see Figure 1-1), total quality management, risk management, and change management. The combinations have produced synergistic results, as illustrated in Figure 1-2.

Figure 1-1   Combination of project management and concurrent engineering.

* DFA = design for assembly
** VMEA = variant mode and effects analysis

Source: Adapted from I. W. Eversheim, Trends and Experience in Using Simultaneous Engineering, *Proceedings of the 1st International Conference on Simultaneous Engineering,* London, December 1990, p. 18.

Figure 1-2   Results of six large corporations using product management in conjunction with other management systems to achieve improvements in product development time.

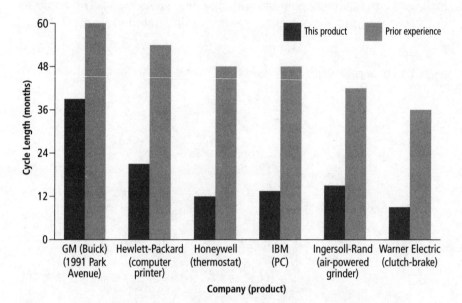

Source: P. G. Smith and D. G. Reinertsen, *Developing Products in Half the Time,* New York: Van Nostrand Reinhold, 1991, p. 2.

Combining project management with concurrent engineering may produce the following benefits.

• New product development time is reduced.
• Average life of the product is increased.
• Sales are increased.
• Revenues are increased.
• The number of customers is increased.

The Department of Defense estimates that concurrent engineering, combined with project management, produces these additional benefits:

- Design changes are reduced by at least 50 percent.
- Product lead times are reduced by more than 50 percent.
- Scrap and rework are reduced by 50 to 75 percent.

Digital Equipment Corporation is a staunch supporter of both project management and concurrent engineering. According to John Hartley, in his book *Concurrent Engineering* (Productivity Press, Cambridge, Massachusetts, 1992, pp. 63, 65), Digital Equipment has identified the following improvements over a three-year period:

- Time to market for new products was reduced from 30 months to 15 months.
- Product costs were reduced by 50 percent.
- Sales increased by 100 percent.
- The break-even point was reached earlier, about six months earlier on average.
- Profitability increased nine to 10 times over what it had been five years before.

Combining project management with total quality management may produce the following benefits:

- Higher product quality
- Happier clients
- Fewer internal and external failures
- Reduced amounts of scrap
- Fewer product recalls and warranty problems

The benefits of combined risk management and project management may include:

- Better risk identification procedures
- Better risk quantification procedures
- Improved processes for responding to risk
- Improved decision-making processes
- Increased tolerance for accepting risk
- Clarified contractual identification of which parties are to bear which risks

Project management combined with change management may yield these benefits:

- The ability to respond to customers' change requests rapidly
- Decreased impact of changes on budget and schedule
- Increased value-added efforts on behalf of the customers
- Good customer relations
- Happier clients

Understanding Project Management

To understand project management, you must first recognize what a project is. A project is an endeavor that has a definable objective, consumes resources, and operates under time, cost, and quality constraints. In addition, projects are generally regarded as activities that may be unique to the company. Any company could manage repetitive activities based on historical standards. The challenge is managing activities that have never been attempted in the past and may never be repeated in the future.

The business world has come to recognize the importance of project management for the future as well as the present. According to Thomas A. Stewart in his 1996 book, *Intellectual Capital: The New Wealth of Organizations* (Doubleday/Currency, New York, p. 207):

> Projects package and sell knowledge. It doesn't matter what the formal blueprint of an organization is—functional hierarchy, matrix, or the emerging process-centered [or horizontal] organization, whose lines of communication and power are drawn along end-to-end business processes.... Routine work doesn't need managers; if it cannot be automated, it can be self-managed by workers. It's the never-ending book of projects—for internal improvement or to serve customers—that creates new value. It draws information together and does something with it—that is, formalizes, captures, and leverages it to produce a higher-values asset.
>
> Consequently, if the old middle managers are dinosaurs, a new class of managerial mammals—project managers—is evolving to fill the

niche they once ruled. Like his biological counterpart, the project manager is more agile and adaptable than the beast he is replacing, more likely to live by his wits than by throwing his weight around.

People who lead or work on winning projects will get the first crack at the next hot gig. The best project managers will seek out the best talent, and the best talent—offered a choice as it often will be—will sign on with the best managers. Seniority matters less than what-have-you-done-for-me-lately....

Not everyone can or should be a project manager, but those who can will be winners. When an organization ceases to be defined by its functional departments, and becomes a portfolio of projects and processes, it's much easier to claim credit for success—the results are obvious. Conversely, it's harder to blame "them" for failure because "they" are on your cross-functional project team.

Effective project management requires extensive planning and coordination. As a result, work flow and project coordination must be managed horizontally, not vertically as in traditional management. In vertical management, workers are organized along top-down chains of command. As a result, they have little opportunity to work with other functional areas. In horizontal management, work is organized across the various functional groups that work with each other. This results in improved coordination and communication among employees and managers.

Horizontal work flow generates productivity, efficiency, and effectiveness. Corporations that have mastered horizontal work flow are generally more profitable than those corporations that continue to use vertical work flow exclusively.

When project managers are required to organize their work horizontally as well as vertically, they learn to understand the operations of other functional units and how functional units interface. This knowledge results in the development of future general managers who understand more of the total operations of their company than their counterparts who came up through a single vertical chain of command.

Project management has become a training ground for future general managers who will be capable of making total business decisions.

No two companies manage projects in the same way. Project management implementation must be based on the culture of the organization. Some organizations have tried to accelerate learning to achieve excellence in project management by creating a center for excellence that constantly benchmarks against the best practices of those companies recognized worldwide. For example, according to Carol Rauh, director of Bellcore's Project Management Center of Excellence:

> Bellcore (Bell Communications Research, Inc.) has been commercializing its business practices.... Project Management certification training was instituted, and the Project Management Center for Excellence (PMCOE) was established to operationalize use of state-of-the-art methods consistently throughout the company. As part of the effort, Bellcore has looked at other companies' practices and has embraced several to enhance our own effectiveness. For example, Bellcore's new opportunity and project review process consists of a series of reviews throughout the project life cycle to ensure profitability and project success by minimizing and controlling risk. Rigorous project management techniques, such as resource loaded networks, quantitative risk management, and technical, schedule, and cost performance measures, are required. The opportunity and project review process, combined with our existing processes, is quickly boosting our Project Management capability.

According to Linda Kretz, president and chief executive officer of 20/20 Solutions, in Atlanta, Georgia, project management as a professional discipline is undergoing significant change. Many companies use the term *project management* to include a number of different functions, some of which might be better described as expediting techniques or command/control management. Real project management differs from these techniques in timing of assignments and authority of the project manager.

Today, most of the managers described as "project managers" are assigned after project planning is complete. Charged with overseeing the implementation or execution of the project, they have no input into the budgeting process and are merely informed about the contractual constraints on the project. They are assigned to the project but are not informed of market analyses or revenue projections for the project. They have no idea how—or even whether—the planned project fits in with the corporation's overall strategic goals. Such concerns, if they are addressed at all, are usually handled by executive managers and held confidential. Ironically, many project managers working today are held accountable for the results of their projects without being privy to critical information. Two questions seem obvious: How accountable can project managers be for fulfilling someone else's plan? And with virtually no control over the project budget, how can they be held responsible for keeping the project on budget and on schedule?

In the future, project managers will be recognized for the value they contribute to the corporation's bottom line. Shooting the messenger will no longer be necessary, because the message will fulfill everyone's expectations. No longer will project managers be informed of the company's financial margin at the end of the fiscal year along with all the other nonexecutive employees of the company. They will be given the authority to address potential problems by proactively managing their projects rather than reacting to ongoing risk factors.

Future project managers will be empowered to act as catalysts for corporate change and quality improvement. They will play central roles in meeting the company's financial goals. Their ability to evaluate the financial justification for projects will be recognized throughout their organizations, and they will be empowered to contribute to feasibility studies and project budgets.

Project Management Life Cycle

Achieving excellence in project management can be accomplished in a few years or a few decades. Excellence can't be achieved without change, and the speed of change is critical. Project management is like total quality management: both are management systems that require extensive education and training. And the educational process must start with senior managers. Why would any employee support change that is not supported from the top down?

Factors such as economic recession, dwindling market share, competition, low profitability, and poor employee morale may drive senior management's commitment to change. Executives must be committed to the change to project management and recognize the value it adds to the corporation before project management can succeed. Ultimately, they must understand that the change to project management will benefit every stakeholder in the company.

Since the early 1990s, the search for excellence in project management has taken on more and more importance. The benefits of project management today are obvious to both customers and contractors. In fact, excellence in project management has become a competitive weapon that attracts new business and retains existing customers.

During the past two decades, the Project Management Institute has grown from 3,000 members to 26,000. The greatest growth has occurred since the late 1980s, probably owing to the certification process established for project personnel. Project management now has a career path. Customers are even requesting that contractors assign certified project managers to their projects. Some companies are offering their employees bonuses of up to $5,000 for passing the national project management certification exam. Even corporate executives are taking the exam with the goal of functioning better as executive project sponsors and exhibiting to customers that their company's senior management supports project management totally.

The life cycle that virtually every company goes through in establishing the foundations for excellence is discussed in detail in Chapters 2 and 3. (The phases of the life cycle are provided in Table 2-1, p. 27.)

The fastest way to establish a foundation for excellence is to implement training and education programs. Table 1-1 displays selected industry types identified by the number of years each company has been using project management and the level of training courses in project management that each offers. Project-driven industries generate most of their income from individual projects. Nonproject-driven industries generate most of their income from products and services. Put another way, non–project-driven industries take on projects that support the organization's products and services; in project-driven industries, the organization exists to support its projects. Some industries are made up of organizations that are not predominantly project-driven but include several divisions that are project-driven. Let's call these hybrid organizations.

Table 1-1.　Amount of project management training offered, by industry types.

		Hybrid	Project-Driven	Project-Driven
High		Automobiles	Automotive subcontractors	Aerospace
		Health care	Computers	Defense
		Machinery	Electronics	Large construction
		Mining		
		Hybrid	**Hybrid**	**Project-Driven**
Medium		Beverages	Banking	Leisure
		Chemicals	Pharmaceuticals	Amusement
		Paper	Oil and gas	Nuclear utilities
			Telecommunications	
		Hybrid	**Hybrid**	**Non-Project-Driven**
Low		Insurance	Food	Commodity Mfg.
		Publishing	Railroads	Metals
		Retail	Tobacco	
		Transportation		
		1–5	5–10	15 or more

LEVEL OF PROJECT MANAGEMENT TRAINING

Years of Project Management Experience

The characteristics of the three types of industries are summarized here:

- The aerospace, defense, and large construction industries are the project-driven stars of yesterday and today. Hundreds of millions of dollars have already been spent in the development of quantitative tools that support project management in these industries. The organizations in these industries prefer to develop their own tools rather than use canned software packages. Several of these companies now enter signed licensing agreements with other companies for the use of their once-proprietary project management software. The project management systems used in these industries are excellent, but their effectiveness is hampered by the formality and number of policies and procedures still in place. The formality of their systems has been driven by their customers, many of them federal agencies.

- The automotive subcontractor, computer, and electronics industries will be the project-driven stars of tomorrow. Several companies in these industries have already achieved excellence in project management. Driven by consumers' demands for greater quality and shorter product development time in the near future, these industries should easily surpass aerospace, defense, and large construction in their project management capabilities. Automotive subcontractors, computer developers, and electronics companies tend to employ young project managers and executives who are willing to accept risk and to reduce the amount of bureaucracy involved in project management.

- Some project-driven companies in the leisure, amusement, and nuclear utility industries have slowly and methodically achieved some degree of excellence in project management. More consistent excellence will be achieved once these industries recognize that they will not be able to survive without fully implementing project management.

- The automotive, health care, machinery, and mining industries are the hybrid stars of today and tomorrow. Although these industries were slow to adopt product management during the 1980s, they are rapidly embracing it now, and many companies have already achieved some level of excellence. Excellence will be attainable for all the companies in these industries once they recognize the effects of changing legislation and new consumer demands. Today, policies and procedures are being streamlined. In addition, subcontractor management practices are being improved significantly, thus fostering trust among contractors and subcontractors. Project management certification is being encouraged.

- Perhaps the most rapid changes in project management are occurring in the banking, pharmaceutical, oil and gas, and telecommunications industries to make them the hybrid stars of tomorrow as well as today. These industries have accomplished more in the past few years than other industries have achieved in 10 years. The need for project management excellence in these rapidly growing industries has been driven by mergers, acquisitions, and legislation. In all likelihood, these industries will surpass others in their ability to use project management as a vehicle for risk assessment.
- Other industries providing a combination of project-driven and non-project-driven products and services are slowly taking up project management, and the need for it has not yet been recognized. These industries include beverages, chemicals, paper, insurance, publishing, retail, transportation, food, railroads, and tobacco. They are often dominated by politics, and projects tend to be driven by schedule and quality concerns. At the end of a project, the project managers in these industries usually have no idea how much money was actually spent.
- The commodity manufacturing and metals industries include predominantly nonproject-driven companies that have very few projects separate from production-driven manufacturing services. The full adoption of project management in these industries may not occur until well into the next century.

Excellence in Project Management

The difference between the average company and the company that has achieved excellence in project management is the way that the growth and maturity phases of the project management life cycle are implemented. Figure 1-3 shows the six areas in which successful companies excel in project management. These six areas are discussed in Chapters 7 through 13. Table 1-2 lists the benefits that companies have enjoyed from practicing project management on a continuous basis.

Figure 1-3   The six components of excellence.

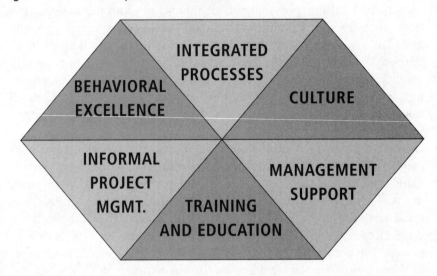

Table 1-2   Attitudes toward project management.

Past View	Present View
Project management requires more people and adds to the overhead costs.	Project management allows us to accomplish more work in less time and with fewer people.
Profitability may decrease.	Profitability will increase.
Project management increases the number of scope changes.	Project management allows better control of scope changes.
Project management creates organizational instability and increases interdepartmental conflict.	Project management makes the organization more efficient and effective through improved organizational behavior.
Project management is really camouflage for the customer's benefit.	Project management allows us to work more closely with our customers.
Project management creates problems.	Project management provides a means for solving problems.
Only large projects need project management.	All projects benefit from project management.

Table 1-2   (continued)

Past View	Present View
Project management decreases quality.	Project management increases quality.
Project management creates power and authority problems.	Project management reduces power struggles.
Project management focuses on suboptimization because it considers only one project.	Project management allows people to make good company decisions.
Project management delivers products.	Project management delivers solutions.
The cost of project management may make the company uncompetitive.	Project management increases business.

Lack of executive buy-in is the principal reason project management so often fails to reach its full potential in some companies. Simply because executives recognize that changes are needed does not mean that change will take place. Executives must realize that success and excellence in project management require decentralization and that executives must surrender critical information and partial control of expenditures to project managers. Because control of information and funding is a source of power for executives, many are reluctant to relinquish all of their power, and they are also reluctant to commit themselves fully to project management.

There are other roadblocks to executive commitment to project management. Some companies still resist the full implementation of project management because they assume that project management is unnecessary. After all, if employees were performing their assignments correctly in the first place, why would project management be needed? Project management is mistakenly dismissed as "checking the checkers." Sometimes it is lumped together with internal auditing.

Professional project managers do not hesitate to tell the full story behind their projects. Unfortunately, this news is not always welcomed by senior managers. It's not what they want to hear. Information takes on a negative aspect given the nature of command control coordination and management. Instead, accurate project information should be accepted as the payoff to proactive professional project management. In the future, senior managers will need to recognize the contributions of project managers in the analysis of market considerations, financial planning, and technical assessments.

Selection of Companies as Examples

More than 200 companies were contacted during the preparation of this book. They were identified through:

- Published literature
- Survey questionnaires
- Privileged knowledge (consulting and lecturing by the author)
- External trainers and consultants

The majority of the companies were provided two sets of questionnaires. Follow-up interviews were then conducted in many instances to verify the quality of the information and to show the interviewees the exact format and context of their responses. Authorization was required for reprinting verbatim quotations from corporate executives and project managers.

The initial intent was to identify at least one or two companies from each major industry without consideration of company size. Many of the companies that have achieved excellence in project management according to my criteria refused to participate. These companies believed that their competitive edge might be compromised by the release of sensitive information.

A second group of companies climbing the ladder to excellence declined participation for fear of being benchmarked against more successful companies in their industries. Some of these organizations recognized from the survey questionnaires that they still have a long way to go to achieve excellence. For example, one executive responded, "We don't do anything you're asking about. Perhaps we should."

A third group initially responded to the surveys but could not secure authorization to release the information. A fourth group of companies that are on track for excellence had second thoughts about seeing their names in print for fear that their customers would have expectations of them higher than they would be able to achieve.

The companies considered in this book as having achieved excellence or as at least being on the right track are these:

Armstrong World Industries	Kinetico, Inc.
Battelle	Lincoln Electric
Bellcore	MCI
BellSouth	Mason & Hanger Corporation
BTR Sealing	Motorola
Centerior Energy	National City Corporation
ChoiceCare	Nortel
Ericsson	OEC Medical Systems
General Electric	Radian International
General Motors	Roadway Express
B. F. Goodrich	Sprint
Hewlett-Packard	Standard Products
ISK Biosciences	United Technologies Automotive
Johnson Controls	USAA
Key Services Corporation	

Small companies have project management cultures that permeate the entire organization. Large companies have pockets of project management. Some pockets may be highly successful in project management while others still have a long way to go. This holds true even for companies that have won the prestigious Malcolm Baldrige Award. Attempts were made to get responses from those divisions that have demonstrated excellence. Similarly, the responses made by individuals do not necessarily reflect the project management practices of the entire company.

Not all companies achieve excellence in all six of the areas shown in Figure 1-3. The companies that have come closest are identified in this book. Some companies identified may excel in two or three components and are included because they are headed in the right direction. These organizations will see the light at the end of the tunnel in the near future.

Unfortunately, there are not many companies that have actually achieved excellence. Roadblocks exist and must be compensated for. Dr. Al Zeitoun, president of the Central Indiana Chapter of the Project Management Institute, believes that:

Project management is here to stay. The world that is going 250 miles an hour with reengineering and continuously changing processes and approaches is making the need for project management and project managers most evident. This group of key players in our organizations will continue to be the only group that can make sense of all these changes and that would maintain the ability [to see] the right amount of details without losing sight of the big picture.

There are, in my opinion, several indicators that project management excellence will have a long way to go:

1. The number of organizations which truly excel in understanding and implementing project management is only a limited few.

2. There are a great number of organizations that talk about project management and have project managers and yet haven't provided the sponsorship required for successful implementation. We are seeing a struggle in defining authority, deliverables, and accountability, just to name a few. There are still myths, such as there's no need for project charters if we have good job descriptions. Organizations are still managing around who they have instead of what needs to be done, and we are still seeing the negotiations for specific people rather than specific deliverables.

3. There is hardly any reasonable level of education and research in project management. Universities, colleges, and institutions are finally coming up with some reasonable programs. Research, however, is barely starting.

4. The standards efforts in project management have a long path to follow. The guide to the PMBOK by the Project Management Institute, among other international bodies of knowledge, provides a solid base for standards. As strong as the document is, there are still several standard issues on the table. One of the key open issues is the global standards issue. What is the global standard going to

be like? Is the recent effort of ISO 10006 a step in the right direction? There is still the crucial need to develop a comprehensive international standard that encompasses all the key disciplines of project management and cuts across industries and global cultures and boundaries.

5. The certification issue has a similar path to follow. On the global side, we have to decide on the need and value of global certification, the proper certification procedure, the certifying body(ies), the recertification requirement, and other multinational complex issues. On the national side, "open issues" concerning the administration of the PMP exam worldwide: whether it's going to be an overall exam that covers all project life cycle phases or stay in the same eight modules format. The ongoing improvement of the points system for certification/recertification will have to continue with the increased concern and demand. Since certification doesn't have a legal implication, are we going to proceed with licensing similar to other professions? Are we going to consider certification and/or licensing based on specific industries? Several open questions still exist.

6. Global cooperation between key project management organizations has only started to be evident. Previous concerns about which organization should take the global leadership, like the challenge between PMI and the International Project Management Association (IPMA) is beginning to subside. The key focus is becoming how can we work together globally to benefit from mutual experiences? For a while the issue of forming a global federation was surfacing.

7. As more and more organizations are beginning to manage their business by projects and rely on the strong cooperation between project managers and resource providers, there is a need for a different skill set for project managers. The mentoring side of a project manager's nature is shining. The need for training that addresses this different set of skills is clear. There is a much greater

need for the soft skills than there is for the hard skills. A continuous improvement effort for training programs will be a requirement for training providers to stay in business.

Based on the previous seven indicators, among several others, I believe that in project management we have only taken the first key steps. We are starting to crawl and will shortly begin to walk, talk, and walk the talk. A strong revolution to truly understand project management and the potential return on investment it can bring is on the way. Organizations will continue to pursue better lessons learned so as to excel in the way projects are managed successfully over and over again. The continued increase in membership of project management organizations and the number of certified professionals will have no limits.

The global scene is going to be where project management excellence will be in greatest demand. Career path for program managers as key individuals for achieving this global excellence will continue to be a very critical issue. Those individuals are going to be strong candidates for the strong senior management seats of the future. Senior managers might actually take back the role of providing the vision that ties their organizations.

Virtual teams will continue to develop, enabling the fast exchange of ideas, minimization of paperwork, and more efficient and effective project work. There is still going to be the need for one-on-one meetings and face-to-face team meetings. This will enable the team to handle key conceptual issues, address hand-off challenges, and solve critical issues.

The true integration of systems and processes will continue to be a strong direction in the global marketplace. Minimizing and/or eliminating redundancy between those systems and processes is the goal of this integration effort. Continuous stream of new project management ideas will appear, and the organizations today, as they become more projectized, will wonder about how strange yesterday was.

Foundations of
Project Management

For every journey, a destination and a travel plan are needed. If the destination is not clearly identified, we can have no idea when the journey is over. To some degree, the same holds true of management practices. We must be able to define what our destination is, what constitutes success, and what constitutes excellence.

Some people contend that to achieve excellence in project management is a continual journey. When the destination is defined in terms of a management process, opportunities for continuous improvement always come forward. However, a framework is still needed if we are to know when our destination is in sight.

Project management is founded on a five-stage life cycle that spans the period between when a company first decides to adopt project management and when it has fully implemented it. Full implementation (or maturity) is not the same as success. And project management excellence goes far beyond both maturity and success. This chapter discusses the project management life cycle, clarifies the definitions of success and excellence, and offers critical success factors as well as critical failure factors as guideposts along the way.

Definition of *Success*

Over the years the definition of project success has changed. In the 1960s, the early days of project management, success was measured entirely in technical terms. Either the product worked or it didn't. In one project I managed during that time, the engineer assigned to perform the work estimated that the work package would take 800 hours to complete. When the work package ultimately took 1300 hours, I asked him why the additional 500 hours were needed. In response, he asked,

"What do you care how much time I spent or how long it took? I got the job done, didn't I?" This type of thinking existed at the time because neither customers nor contractors felt any pressure to contain costs. Cost control was an abstract concept, not a reality.

As contractors began to understand project management better and stronger cost control became a requirement, the definition of success changed. Success came to be defined as accomplishing the effort on time, within budget, and at an acceptable level of quality. But even that updated definition was still incomplete.

The literature on project management started to accumulate during the early 1980s. Articles described successful projects and lessons learned. Contractors began modeling their project management processes after published success stories under the mistaken belief that what worked for one company would work equally well for theirs. This misconception was further reinforced when companies achieved success on one or two projects and concluded incorrectly that they had found a management panacea.

A 1985 paper I coauthored with David Cleland, Ph.D., identified some of the factors common to successful projects. Hindsight has proven, however, that the results we reported were more indicative of experience than of success or excellence. The problems with our research were twofold. First, the research was conducted during the early 1980s, before publications describing numerous successful projects appeared. Second, and perhaps more important, several executives we surveyed said that they considered less than 10 percent of the completed projects to be successfully managed even though the projects' ultimate objectives had been achieved.

Any project can be driven to success through executive meddling, brute force, and big sticks. This by no means should be taken to mean that a successfully completed project is the result of excellence in project management.

A Better Definition of *Success*

The problem with defining success as on time, within budget, and at the desired level of quality is the internal focus of the definition. The ultimate customer should have some say in deciding whether or not the project is successful. Today, the definition of success is stated in terms of five factors:

- Completed on time
- Completed within budget
- Completed at the desired level of quality
- Accepted by the customer
- Resulted in customer allowing contractor to use customer as a reference.

Project managers and their managers now accept that project quality is determined by the customer, not the contractor. The same is true for project success. Today, a contractor can complete a project on time, within budget, and within quality limits, and still the project may not be accepted by the customer. The ultimate definition of success may very well be that it occurs only when the customer is so pleased with the results that the customer allow the contractor to use the customer's name as a reference.

Other Definitions of Success

The definition of success can also change based on whether or not the company is project driven. In a project-driven company, the entire business of the company is based in fulfilling projects under contract with external customers. In nonproject-driven companies, however, projects exist to support ongoing product or service production. The definition of success in nonproject-driven companies includes the completion of projects without disturbing ongoing internal business activities. In such businesses, it is possible, therefore, to complete projects within time, budget, and quality standards and, at the same time, cause irrevocable damage to the overall organization. This damage results when executive managers and project managers forget that their projects must always be secondary in importance to the company's ongoing business.

It is important to remember that all companies do not have the same standards for defining success. A brewery in Venezuela defines a successful project as one that falls within its predetermined time, cost, quality, and scope limitations. Disney decides project success is fulfilling its time, cost, quality, and safety requirements, with safety the most important requirement. Brian Vannoni of General Electric's Plastic Group defines success this way: "The technical aspects, timing and costs [in the past] were the three critical areas of performance measurement for our project managers. In today's world, that is not sufficient. We have to also be concerned with environmental and safety regulations, quality, customer satisfaction, and … productivity [of] manufacturing operations. So a project now has at least eight measurables and critical parameters that we gauge success around."

Successful companies measure success both externally, by using critical success factors, and internally, by referring to key performance indicators. Critical success factors are those needed to produce the desired deliverables for the customer. These critical success factors are typical.

- Adherence to schedules
- Adherence to budgets
- Adherence to quality standards
- Appropriateness and timing of sign-offs
- Adherence to change control processes
- Accomplishment of contract add-ons

Critical success factors measure end results. Key performance indicators, on the other hand, measure the ongoing quality of the processes involved in achieving the desired end results. Another way to say this is that key performance indicators are internal measures that can be reviewed on a periodic basis throughout the entire life cycle of the project. Typical key performance indicators include:

- Consistent use of project management systems
- Establishment of control processes
- Use of interim metrics
- Quality of resources used versus resources planned
- Involvement of the customer

Project Management Life Cycle

By the end of the project management life cycle, a company is experienced enough to establish fully developed and repetitive systems and processes. These processes and systems mean that it is highly probable that every new project will be successfully managed. Repetitive processes and systems do not, however, guarantee success. They simply increase the probability of success.

Table 2-1 shows the phases of the project management life cycle. Virtually every company that achieves some level of project management expertise has gone through these phases. The culture of each organization and the nature of its business dictate the amount of time spent in each phase.

Table 2-1.   The five phases of the project management life cycle.

Embryonic	Executive Management Acceptance	Line Management Acceptance	Growth	Maturity
Recognize need	Get visible executive support	Get line management support	Recognize life cycle changes	Develop a management cost/schedule control system
Recognize benefits	Achieve executive understanding of project management	Achieve line management commitment	Develop a project management system	Integrate cost and schedule control
Recognize applications	Establish project sponsorship	Provide line management education	Make the commitment to planning	Develop an educational program to enhance project management skills
Recognize what must be done	Become willing to change way of doing business	Become willing to release employees for project management training	Minimize creeping scope Select a project tracking system	

Phase 1: Embryonic

In the embryonic phase, both middle and senior managers recognize the need for, the benefits of, and the applications of project management. This recognition is more than giving lip service by saying that project management should be used to achieve project objectives. Senior managers especially must understand that success as well as failure in project management directly affects the bottom line. In my 35 years of experience in project management, I have yet to find even one company anywhere in the world that has implemented project management and then given it up. The reason? It works.

Once executives and managers come to realize that the success or failure of project management will affect their organization's survivability in today's competitive world economy, the development of project management systems accelerates. Unfortunately, it may take months or even years for managers to recognize project management's true effect on the bottom line. For example, after I had been providing product management training for employees at the Timken Company in Canton, Ohio, for three years, one of Timken's directors asked me to explain why the company should continue funding the training courses. The director said that he had not seen any return on the investment of training dollars. During the meeting, however, the director did come to realize that Timken was realizing or at least getting closer to achieving its project objectives. The company was receiving more concise and accurate reports, and he himself was seeing fewer conflicts come up to him for top-level resolution. This director had been so involved in the projects that he didn't see the changes that had occurred over the past three years. But when he was asked to step back and look at the big picture, he had to admit the value the training courses yielded.

Phase 2: Executive Management Acceptance

The second phase in the life cycle is executive management acceptance. In Phase 2, it is critical that executives visibly demonstrate their support for product management. The key factor is visibility.

For example, in one large appliance manufacturer, the senior executives attended a one-week retreat conducted at a site outside the company. The goal of the retreat was to identify the strategic initiatives needed to remain competitive at the turn of the century and beyond. By the end of the meeting, 20 strategic initiatives had been identified. Third on the list was project management. When the executives returned to their offices, they sent out memos to all the managers who reported to them that emphasized the importance of effective project management. The middle managers filed their memos in the usual places (the trash can, for some) and did not take them seriously. The middle managers recognized lip service when they heard it and knew that no changes or management support would be forthcoming.

The middle managers did make attempts over the next three years to develop a one-hour executive briefing on what senior managers could do to accelerate implementing project management in their company. But the executive briefing never took place because the executives found excuse after excuse to explain why they were unable to attend the briefing. This lack of interest only reinforced the middle managers' belief that there was no real support for project management on the executive level.

How can executives persuade nonexecutive employees that the executives understand and support project management? Perhaps the best way is for executives to act as project sponsors. Acting as a project sponsor demonstrates support for project management systems as well as specific projects.

A lack of visible executive management support is the primary reason behind project failures. During the 1980s and early 1990s, the telecommunications industry struggled with achieving successful project management without having visible executive support. In telecommunications, the top levels of management were rewarded for their political astuteness to the point that promotions and assignments were based on internal politics. As a result, senior managers were very reluctant to act as project sponsors, given their fear of losing their political positions if they sponsored a project that failed. Fortunately for individual executives and telecommunications in general, this mind-set is now changing, though at a slow pace.

Finally, in Phase 2 senior managers must be willing to lead the way when extensive changes are necessary in their organization. By what they do and say, they must display a real commitment to changing the way the organization does business. Senior managers must be willing to take charge of the change process, to explain the reasons for change, and to clearly describe the new expectations they have of employees.

Phase 3: Line Management Acceptance

The third phase in the project management life cycle is line management support. The biggest obstacle to gaining line managers' support is a lack of executive management support for project management. Few line managers would eagerly accept and support project management if they knew their superiors would not support it.

Line managers do not necessarily need a strong understanding of project management tools, but they must be trained in the principles of project management. (The basics of modern project management are discussed in Chapter 6.) After all, the line managers are responsible for releasing employees for project management training and eventually assigning staff to project teams.

Phase 4: Growth

The fourth phase is growth in the number of projects being managed. This phase may coincide with the first three phases, even the embryonic phase, or run in parallel to them. However, the first three phases must be complete before Phase 4 can be considered complete.

Senior managers' knowledge and support of project management can accelerate the completion of the growth phase. One example is Choice-Care of Cincinnati, Ohio, perhaps one of the best health management organizations in the United States. During a recent video conference on project management, ChoiceCare's vice president for information systems, Byron Smith, explained what senior management had done in his organization to build a successful project management system. "Senior management at ChoiceCare believes that it is critical for us to take advantage of as many opportunities [as possible].... As a relatively small organization, we have approximately 500 associates. We believe that means we need to leverage project management capabilities throughout our entire organization, and that we, in fact, need to take advantage of the skills and talents of all our associates." ChoiceCare has taken these steps:

- It created a standard process for its teams to follow.
- It developed a series of cross-functional steering teams organized around the company's most strategic initiatives. The role of each team is to provide guidance to its assigned project initiative. This

allows senior managers enough time to sponsor a large number of projects rather than working hands-on with only a few projects.
• It clearly defined its corporate values and required behaviors. These values and behaviors allow individual employees to understand how decisions are made and how they should interact with other team members and coworkers assigned to other projects.

Christine Dombrowski, a director at ChoiceCare, also explained that having a team management model has clarified roles and responsibilities. By following the team model, team members and project stakeholders can know what to expect of each other and when.

ChoiceCare also requires significant project management training. More than 25 percent of associates have been trained in project management, and that 25 percent includes executive managers. Included in the training are interpersonal skills building and team skills building.

During the growth phase, project management systems are developed and refined for control and standardization. Such systems reflect a company's commitment to quality and planning as well as the need to minimize scope changes (also called scope creep). Scope creep sometimes occurs during the planning or execution of a project, most often during execution. Scope creep results when features or functions are added to the project. Such changes drive up costs and lengthen the schedule. Although most scope creep changes are small, added together they can endanger the project. You might say that scope creep can happen when you are building a new home. Each design change made after construction has started adds to the cost of the house as well as how long it will take to build.

There is a mistaken belief, especially among young project managers, that perfect planning can be achieved, thus eliminating scope creep. In excellent companies, scope creep is expected and planned for. According to Frank T. Anbari, project manager of technical systems for the National Railroad Passenger Corporation (Amtrak):

> Scope definition is extremely important to the success of any project. Scope "creep" and scope "leap" are often the root cause of project failure. That much we know. However, in some projects, it is extremely difficult, if not impossible, to have complete definition of project scope before execution is started. This is particularly true in

the case of high, new, and emerging technologies projects, such as telecommunications and information technology, as opposed to more stable disciplines, such as certain projects in manufacturing and construction. The customer may not be able to visualize the organization's needs and to what extent these needs can be satisfied. Technological advances may surpass implementation pace. Devices originally envisioned and selected in project design may become obsolete, or even unavailable, due to the introduction of more advanced models.

In such cases, it may become imperative to plan the project "from the middle out." This requires heavy involvement of the customer/user in initial project definition, general planning, design, and prototype development. Flexibility and adaptability become essential in project execution to accommodate changes in technology, refinements of requirements, and project replanning. To succeed in these projects, it is important to pull the "middle" of the project to the earliest possible time. This can be accomplished by profound understanding of the business needs of the customer and by helping the customer understand current and expected technological capabilities. Yet, even with this approach, scope creep is still possible.

The final activity in the growth phase is selecting a project planning and control software package. During the 1970s and 1980s, companies spent millions of dollars developing their own computer software packages for project management. Today, the quality of off-the-shelf packages available leaves no reason for individual companies to create their own software. One of the best, if not the best, is Microsoft Project. The Ford Motor Company recently contracted with Microsoft to custom design Microsoft Project for its specific use.

Sooner or later, most companies that take on project management finish the first four phases of the cycle. One or two years is a reasonable time frame for aggressive companies to reach the growth phase. The maturity phase is another story.

Phase 5: Maturity

To reach the maturity phase, a company must understand the importance of integrating time and cost management. Without such integration, no one can determine the status of a project just by looking at the schedule or the budget. Time and cost monitoring must become two parts of the same activity.

In a large division of one of the big three automakers in Detroit, the cost-control people sat on one side of the building and the schedule people sat on the other side. The cost people had no idea what the schedule was, the schedule people had no idea what the budget was, and nobody had any idea what the real status of the project was. Spending 30 percent of the budget does not mean that the project is 30 percent complete. And completing 30 percent of the work does not mean that 30 percent of the budget has been spent.

Integrating time and cost monitoring is not easy. It requires a total revamping of the cost-accounting system to include earned value measurement. It also requires an accurate determination of how much money is being spent on each activity (emphasize the accurate). Because most employees are reluctant to support accounting systems that require daily time cards, an integrated system is often unpopular, at least at first. Employees resent time cards because they make them feel as though Big Brother is watching. And cost-accounting personnel are notoriously resistant to change of any kind. Change means learning new computer systems and new processes. It may even mean a change in culture. Cost accountants can come up with a thousand excuses why the organization should not implement earned value measurement.

During the early 1980s, I was invited to consult for RJR Tobacco Company (now RJR-Nabisco). The company had laid out plans to spend more than $2 billion to double its cigarette production capacity. When I asked one of the company's vice presidents why they needed my consulting services, he said, "The last capital project we managed came in 20 percent below budget. What happens if we come in 20 percent *over* budget instead? Over budget by 20 percent on $2 billion is a lot of money." Well, I had never heard of a capital project that came in 20 percent *below* budget, and didn't know what to say. The vice president picked up the phone and asked the procurement people to gather together all of the purchase requisitions for the materials used in the below-budget project. What would I have learned from those? I then asked to see instead calculations of the direct labor hours. The vice president informed me that in RJR's Winston-Salem plant, most employees, especially the white-collar workers, did not fill out time cards. Then I had to ask whether it was possible that the project actually came in 20 percent *over* budget due to labor cost overruns and the company simply did not realize it. After all, how could a manufacturer of cigarettes or anything else create meaningful budgets for future projects when it cannot determine how much it really spent on previous projects. Today, RJR employees fill out time cards.

The last element of the maturity phase is the development of a long-term educational program. Without a sustained educational program, an organization may revert to old practices very quickly. Long-term educational programs that support project management demonstrate the organization's commitment to project management.

The most effective educational programs are those based on documented records of the lessons learned on previous projects. In successful organizations, every project team is required to prepare such lessons-learned files. The lessons learned then are integrated in the training program.

Without access to documented lessons learned, any company can quickly revert from the maturity phase to an immature phase. Knowledge is lost, and past mistakes are repeated.

Is it possible to complete the maturity phase of the project management life cycle without having gone through the other phases? Some say that it is possible, but it's definitely not usual. If a company has completed the maturity phase effectively, it will be able to answer yes to the following questions.

- Has your company adopted a project management system and used it consistently?
- Has it implemented a philosophy that drives it toward project management success?
- Has your company made a serious commitment to project planning at the onset of each new project?

- Has it minimized the number of scope changes by committing itself to realistic objectives?
- Does it recognize that cost and schedule control are inseparable?
- Has your company selected the right people as project managers?
- Do executive managers receive project sponsor–level information rather than too much project manager–level information?
- Have executives strengthened the involvement of line managers and supported their efforts?
- Does your company focus on deliverables rather than resources?
- Does it cultivate and reward effective communication, cooperation, teamwork, and trust?
- Do senior managers share recognition for successful projects with the entire project team and line managers?
- Does your company focus on identifying and solving problems early, quickly, and cost-effectively?
- Do project staff use project management software as a tool rather than as a substitute for effective planning and interpersonal communications?
- Has your company instituted an all-employee training program based on documented lessons learned?

Critical Factors in Project Management

Table 2-1 listed the critical success factors for achieving a fully developed project management system. Critical failure factors that create obstacles to effective project management are just as informative. Typical critical failure factors are listed in Table 2-2.

Table 2-2.   Critical factors in project management life cycle.

Critical Success Factors	Critical Failure Factors
Executive Management Acceptance Stage	
Consider employee recommendations	Refuse to consider ideas of associates
Recognize that change is necessary	Unwilling to admit that change may be necessary

Table 2-2.   (continued)

Critical Success Factors	Critical Failure Factors
Executive Management Acceptance Stage (continued)	
Understand the executive role in project management	Believe that project management control belongs at executive levels
Line Management Acceptance Stage	
Willing to place company interest before personal interest	Reluctant to share information
Willing to accept accountability	Refuse to accept accountability
Willing to see associates advance	Not willing to see associates advance
Growth Stage	
Recognize the need for corporatewide systems	View a standard system as a threat rather than as a benefit
Support uniform status monitoring/reporting	Fail to understand the benefits of project management
Recognize the importance of effective planning	Provide only lip service to planning
Maturity Stage	
Recognize that cost and schedule are inseparable	Believe that project status can be determined from schedule alone
Track actual costs	See no need to track actual costs
Develop project management training	Believe that growth and success in project management are the same

Definition of *Excellence*

An experienced company can used project management routinely and for years and still not achieve excellence in project management. An organization that practices project management is not guaranteed that excellence will follow automatically. The last phase in the life cycle may be based on repetitive practices or rigid policies and procedures. It may be achieved when all employees simply understand their job descriptions. The definition of project management *excellence* must extend well beyond experience and success. Organizations excellent in project management create an environment in which there exists a *continuous* stream of successfully managed projects, where success is measured by having achieved performance that is in the best interest of the whole company as well as a specific project.

First part of *Excellence* Defined

Let's break down this definition. First, excellence in project management requires a continuous stream of successfully managed projects. This in no way implies that the projects are successful, just that the projects were successfully managed. Remember: successful implementation of project management does not guarantee that individual projects will be successful. As Figure 2-1 indicates, companies excellent in project management still have their share of project failures. Should a company find that 100 percent of their projects are successful, then that company is not taking enough business risks. That's to say, excellent companies take risks; they simply know which risks are worth taking and which are not. (Risk management is discussed in Chapter 7.)

Figure 2-1   Success against time.

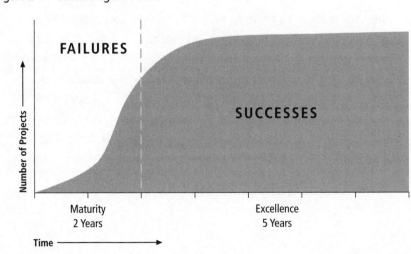

Early termination of a project, under the right circumstances, can be viewed as successful when the resources initially dedicated to that project are reassigned to more profitable activities or the technology needed for that project does not exist and cannot be invented cost-effectively within a reasonable time period.

Second Part of *Excellence* Defined

The second part of the definition requires that decisions made on individual projects must take into account the best interest of both the project and the company as a whole. Take the case of a project manager who fights for the best resources available, knowing full well that his or her project has been assigned an extremely low priority. Companies excellent in project management develop cultures in which project managers are taught and encouraged to make decisions based on sound business judgment and not internal parochialism.

Companies that have achieved excellence in project management also realize that excellence is ongoing. Complacency opens doors for the competition.

Chris Hansen, director of research and development for Kinetico, has this comment on the need for continuous improvement in project management:

Project management never stops. It can always [get] better. We've put procedures into place that we've never used before. To be successful and competitive and to meet market needs on a timely basis, this is the only way our company will survive. People in our company are being educated about the benefits [of project management excellence] and are becoming more positive. They are trying harder to work together as a team. They know it is the best way to accomplish our goal.

Chapter 3

Driving Forces

When a company decides to implement project management, both senior and middle managers must recognize the need for project management and share a passion for making it work. Simply using project management processes and tools, even frequently, does not guarantee that effective project management will become a permanent way of doing business.

Fortunately, several driving forces push organizations toward success in project management. The driving forces originate with real business problems and opportunities that need to be addressed through solid business practices.

This chapter discusses the seven most common forces behind the successful implementation of project management:

- Capital projects
- Consumers' expectations
- Internal competition
- Executive managers' buy-in
- New product development
- Efficiency and effectiveness
- Company survival

Capital Projects

Even the smallest manufacturing organization may spend millions of dollars each year on capital projects. Large, international conglomerates regularly spend billions. Without effective estimation practices and cost and schedule control, capital projects can strap an organization's cash flow and even force the organization to lay off employees when capital equipment is not available on schedule or is installed improperly. In nonproject-driven services and manufacturing companies especially, internal capital projects alone are reason enough to adopt project management permanently.

Lincoln Electric

Sometimes it takes capital projects for a company that is manufacturing oriented to recognize the need for project management. General Electric's Lamp Division and Tungsten Division realized this in the early 1980s as the number of capital projects increased. Another example is a company that embarks on a massive capital project that is larger than any it's attempted in the past, as in the case of Lincoln Electric.

Lincoln Electric is a medium-size manufacturer of electric motors, in Cleveland, Ohio. All of its projects are performed for internal customers, and the projects range in value from $10,000 to $30 million. Because the size of its projects was growing, the company needed a better project management system. According to Jim Nelson, senior plant engineer at Lincoln Electric:

> The $30 million motor department expansion was so large and complex that better control was needed. After a slow, more "seat-of-the-pants" start, a professional scheduler was hired and a more project management atmosphere was created.

Other factors drove the changes in project management.

- Deadlines had already been set, and management wanted reliable information on the progress being made in meeting those objectives.
- The number of simultaneous activities required organization to coordinate overlapping responsibilities.
- Costs needed to be monitored and controlled.

Asked to describe the lessons learned from this project, Nelson said:

> Most of the projects that I worked on throughout my career here at Lincoln Electric were my own projects. I believe that I've learned from critical self-evaluation and have formed strong opinions

throughout the years about how projects should be run. The EP3 project, which I managed, gave me the opportunity to expand those opinions on a grand scale. I believe that this project was one of the best organized that I have worked on at Lincoln Electric, and the best organized that Lincoln Electric has ever had. I believe that the main reason for success was that I spent a lot of time gathering and disseminating information to the right people, who then had the authority to make their own intelligent decisions, as long as the general guidelines were being followed.

Customers' Expectations

Customers' expectations can be another driving force. Today, customers expect contractors not only to deliver a quality product or quality services, but also to manage this activity using sound project management practices. This includes effective periodic reporting of status, timely reporting of status, and overall effective customer communications. It should be no surprise that low bidders may not be rewarded contracts because of poor project management practices on previous projects undertaken for the client.

Hewlett-Packard Company

For example, Hewlett-Packard Company has mastered consumers' expectations. Between 1988 and 1994, revenue at Hewlett-Packard doubled. During that period, and especially in 1992, the company's worldwide customer support system recognized that customers' needs were becoming increasingly customized and complex. Customers needed smooth transitions as they implemented new communication environments, and they looked to their vendors to provide total solutions. Support services were becoming more critical and came to be viewed as key factors in winning both the product and support orders.

Hewlett-Packard's management decided to expand its customer support sales organization and focus support resources on the development of excellence in project management. A new group responsible for dedicated project resources was formed within the support organization and was given the charter to become professional project management experts. The group was at its onset and remains today composed of individuals who have extensive backgrounds in field service, including technical support and problem management.

At the same time, Hewlett-Packard established an aggressive project management training program as well as an informal mentor program. The mentor program allowed seasoned project managers to provide guidance and direction to newly assigned colleagues.

In addition to the existing internal training courses, new project management courses were developed. Where necessary, these courses were supplemented with external programs providing comprehensive education in all aspects of project management. Efforts to achieve industry-recognized certification in project management became a critical initiative for the group.

The company recognized that it could expand its business by demonstrating superior project management skills. In large, complex solution implementations, project management was viewed as a differentiator in the sales process. Satisfied customers were becoming loyal customers. The result was additional support and product business for Hewlett-Packard. The company also recognized that its customers either didn't have or didn't want to tie up their own resources, and Hewlett-Packard was able to educate customers in the value of professional project management.

According to Jim Hansler, a project manager at Hewlett-Packard, the following benefits were obtained:

> First, we are meeting the implementation needs of our customers at a lower cost than they can achieve. Second, we are able to provide our customers a consistent means of implementing and delivering a project through the use of a common set of tools, processes, and project methodologies. Third, we are leveraging additional sales using project management. Our customers now say, "Let HP do it!"

Internal Competition

The third common driving force behind project management is internal competition. Some companies become so complacent in the way they conduct their ongoing business that the organization soon realizes that it may be cheaper to outsource pieces of production or services such as management information systems. In such situations, it is a rude awakening when internal units find themselves in competition with outside sources. To make matters worse, the functional unit facing the challenge may attempt to protect itself by insulating itself from other functional units. This serves only to increase the level of internal competition for the sake of survival.

Centerior Energy

For example, internal competition may affect the information systems division of a company. When senior managers realize that the information systems project could be completed at lower cost, higher quality, and less time externally, they may opt for outsourcing. Centerior Energy's story illustrates this point.

Centerior Energy's Adrian Lammi commented on the difficulties that Centerior Energy faced between 1993 and 1995 when it attempted to use project management for information systems projects rather than outsourcing them:

> Two prior attempts to implement a standard application-development methodology had failed. Although our new director of information systems aggressively supported this third effort by mandating the use of a standard methodology and standard tools, significant obstacles were still present.

> The learning curve for the project management methodology was high, resulting in a tendency of the [project leaders] to impose their own interpretations on methodology tasks rather than learn the documented explanations. This resulted in an inconsistent interpretation of the methodology, which in turn produced inconsistencies when [we tried to use] previous estimates in estimating new projects.

Ultimately, the people in Centerior Energy's information systems division realized that the division's continued existence might very well be based on how well and how fast it could develop an effective project management system. By 1997, the sense of urgency had affected everyone in the division, and project management was firmly established. The division is now competing successfully against other external organizations. According to Lammi:

> We now offer project management services as an option in our service level agreements with our corporate "customers." One success story involved a project to implement a new corporate identity, in which various components across the corporation were brought together. The project was able to cross department boundaries and maintain an aggressive schedule. The process of defining tasks and estimating their durations resulted in a better understanding of the requirements of the project. This in turn provided accurate estimates that drove significant decisions regarding the scope of the project in light of severe budget pressures. Project decisions tended to be based on sound business alternatives rather than raw intuition. Although the project was eventually suspended because of an impending merger, project sponsors and participants agreed the project management process was a success and had produced a plan that could be truly implemented.

Executive Managers' Buy-In

A fourth driving force toward excellence is executive buy-in. Visible executive support can reduce the impact of many obstacles. Typical obstacles that can be overcome through executive support include:

- Line managers who do not support the project
- Employees who do not support the project
- Employees who believe that project management is just a fad
- Employees who do not understand how the business will benefit
- Employees who do not understand customers' expectations
- Employees who do not understand the executives' decision

Roadway Express

In the spring of 1992, Roadway Express realized that its support systems (specifically its information management systems) needed to be upgraded. Rapid changes in technology demanded ongoing change. Mike Wickham, the company's president, was a strong believer in continuous improvement. Several projects were being undertaken at that time, demanding a significantly larger amount of resources than previous projects had. The new projects also required effective cooperation between functional departments.

Non–executive-level employees at Roadway had minimal knowledge of project management tools and processes in 1992. Executive managers, however, understood and accepted project management.

Roadway Express decided to use project management on a two-year project that had executive visibility and support and was considered strategically important to the company. The president of Roadway Express recognized the difficulty of quick project management implementation on a large project, but he was willing to accept the risk. Three problems troubled the project at the onset. (1) The project needed a full-time manager, but the company chose to appoint a line manager to serve as project manager. (2) There was virtually no knowledge of project management beyond the executive offices. And (3) the company used project management sporadically rather than continuously.

The line manager's assignment involved doing two jobs at once and for two years: managing his line and managing the new project. After three months, the line manager appointed originally resigned as project manager, giving as reasons stress and his inability to manage his line effectively. A second line manager was appointed on a part-time basis, but he also found it necessary to resign. The company then assigned a third line manager, but this time it released the manager from all of her line responsibility for the duration of the project.

Problems continued. After three months, the project manager complained that some of her team members were very unhappy about taking on project management and were threatening to resign. They were ready to leave the company to get away from project management. The line manager also reported that the team had met every deliverable and milestone so far. It was apparent to the president and officers of the company that project management was working. Their task became persuading the disgruntled employees that their work was important and that the company appreciated their efforts.

The president himself assumed the role of project sponsor. By becoming the project sponsor, he made it clear that project management was there to stay at Roadway Express. He instituted project management training programs and appeared at each new session. The company also clearly delineated the role of the project manager from the role of the line manager, as shown in Table 3-1.

Table 3-1.   Project manager's responsibilities versus line manager's responsibilities.

Project Manager's Responsibilities	Line Manager's Responsibilities
Define the scope of the project	Manage resources
Identify line areas that contribute to project success	Estimate costs
Identify costs and benefits	Commit to deliverables
Get approvals	Manage ongoing line responsibilities
Monitor and report on progress	Report status on a regular basis
Manage identification and resolution of problems	Report variances immediately
Negotiate scope deliverables	Identify cross-functional requirements and provide functional and technical expertise
Control changes to avoid creeping scope	Identify and resolve problems
Plan and schedule user training	Assist in development of test, training, implementation, and support plans
Ensure the development of user's manuals and training materials	
Plan and carry out testing and data verification	
Plan final implementation	
Plan for postimplementation user support	
Provide input to the line manager on the performance of team members	
Declare the project done	

The very visible support demonstrated by the president affected every area of the company. Roadway Express in eight months had accomplished what it takes other companies two or three years to achieve, thanks to executive buy-in from the start. According to President Mike Wickham:

> Project management, no matter how sophisticated or how well trained, cannot function effectively unless all line management is committed to a successful project outcome. Before we put our current process in place, we actively involved all those line managers who thought it was their job to figure out all the reasons a system WOULD NEVER WORK! Now, the steering committee says, "This is the project. Get behind it and see that it works." It is a much more efficient use of resources when everyone is focused on the same goals.

New Product Development

Another driving force behind project management is new product development. The development of a new product can take months or years and may well be the main source of the company's income for years to come. The new product development process encompasses the time it takes to develop, commercialize, and introduce new products to the market. By applying the principles of project management to new product development, a company can produce more products in a shorter period of time, at lower cost than usual, with a potentially high level of quality and still satisfy the needs of the customer.

ISK Biosciences Corporation

ISK Biosciences Corporation is a worldwide manufacturer and marketer of agricultural and specialty chemicals. It implemented project management both formally and informally in manufacturing and capital projects during the 1980s. When the company purchased ISK Japan in 1992, managers had to revisit its new product development system.

At the time it was purchased, ISK Japan had several experimental compounds ready to be developed for use in the Americas. The norm in the chemical industry was to bring a new compound to market over 8 to 10 years at a cost of between $40 million and $60 million dollars. To accommodate ISK Japan's new products, ISK Biosciences developed a new product development process on the basis of formal project management. Project managers were assigned for the three world distribution areas targeted: North and South America, Europe, and Asia. Michael Peplowski, corporate quality facilitator, explains the three major factors involved in the new system:

> (1) We used a stage-gate system to help manage risk and add discipline to the process. (2) We put heavy reliance on software [Microsoft Project] to help us develop the aggregate plan whereby we identify strategy and resources available versus capability. (3) We now pay close attention to details.

The company experienced the following benefits from applying project management systems to new product development projects:

- Decreased cycle time and lower costs
- Realistic plans with greater potential for meeting development time frames
- Better communication about what is expected from work groups and when
- Feedback about lessons learned on the project

Efficiency and Effectiveness

Improvement in overall effectiveness and efficiency of the company is difficult. It often requires change in the corporate culture, and culture changes are always painful. The speed at which such changes accelerate the implementation of project management often depends on the size of the organization. The larger the organization, the slower the change.

Kinetico Inc.

Kinetico Inc. is a relatively small and privately held company that has successfully implemented project management. It competes within the highly competitive water treatment industry. The company was started in 1970 by two engineers, whose influence is still evident in the heavy engineering/technical approach taken in their high-quality and innovative products. Kinetico's products are among the most expensive in the industry and are widely regarded to be of the highest quality on the market. The company has three core divisions: the Consumer Products Division, the Engineered Systems Division, and the Community Water Systems Division.

This discussion will focus on the Consumer Products Division, which has about 200 employees. The division manufactures residential water treatment products, which are designed, manufactured, and shipped at one location.

One of Kinetico's greatest strengths is its strong corporate culture, instilled from the beginning. The owners to this day insist on a family-type atmosphere, which is shown by its policies on employee education and promotion from within. Project management at Kinetico is based on an informal approach. The culture seems to allow for good relationships among employees and encourages teamwork.

During the 1980s, Kinetico began to grow, and departmentalized management began to change. The company went into a phase of "pass it on"-style project management, which can be considered linear engineering compared to the concurrent engineering used today. The projects were broken down into elements. When one particular department finished its tasks, it would pass the project on to the next department. This system caused obvious problems, such as lack of efficiency that resulted in redundancy of work. Projects consistently finished over budget and behind schedule.

A formal project management system emerged in the 1990s. The inefficiency of projects during the 1980s led to the hiring of managers who had experience in project management. Project teams now are headed by experienced project leaders. Teams usually consist of one or more members from each of the functional areas: usually, marketing, manufacturing, engineering, legal, quality, research and development, compliance, accounting, and purchasing.

During the past 25 years, Kinetico has gone through some very distinct stages of project management and made mistakes that have taught a number of lessons. The various stages were the results of problems that forced the company to change. According to Chris Hansen, the director of research and development at Kinetico:

> The mass of confusion [resulting from earlier project management systems resulted in] wasted time, wasted energy, and wasted resources.... So we created a new program and organized a project flow that not only fit the management style [and the company's traditional corporate culture], but also fit our manufacturing capabilities.... We developed, introduced, and implemented the program and communicated to people that this program is very flexible.... We have made a lot of changes and adjustments to it from people's input. We are always after input and continually state that if something becomes too cumbersome, difficult, or if something doesn't make sense, we are flexible to change. That is a point that has to be executed; you have to be able to meet change. Things change every day. You have to be able to adapt. We're going to get faster and better.

Company Survival

Obviously, the most powerful force behind project management excellence is survival. It could be argued that all of the other forces are tangential to survival. (See Figure 3-1.) In some industries, such as aerospace and defense, poor project management can quickly lead to going out of business. Smaller companies, however, certainly are not immune.

Defcon Corporation

One defense contractor (which asked that its case be disguised; we'll call it Defcon for convenience) had survived for almost 20 years on fixed-price, lump-sum government contracts. A characteristic of fixed-price contracts is that the customer does not audit the contractor's books, costs, or even its project management system. As a result, the company managed its projects rather loosely between 1967 and 1987. As long as deliverables were available on time, the capabilities of the project management system were never questioned.

Figure 3-1   The components of survival.

But by 1987, the government subcontracting environment had changed significantly, for several reasons:

- The Department of Defense was undergoing restructuring.
- The cutbacks in defense spending were predicted to get even worse.
- The department was giving out more and more cost-reimbursable contracts.
- The department was pressuring contractors to restructure from traditional to product-oriented organizational forms.
- The department was also pressuring contractors to reduce costs, especially overhead rates.
- The department was demanding higher quality products.

- The department began requiring that contractors demonstrate better project management practices in their proposals.

Simply to survive, Defcon needed to bid on cost-reimbursable contracts. Internally, this required two critical changes. First, the company needed to adopt more formal project management systems. Second, it needed to learn how to measure and report earned value. To win cost-reimbursable government contracts, the contractor was required to gain government validation of its earned value cost-control and reporting system.

A manager at another defense contractor that survived the changes in the defense spending environment by implementing stronger project management systems after 1987 said:

> After system validation in 1987, it took six months to a year to properly train and develop the skills needed in cost [accounting] managers and work package supervisors. As you moved along in the program, there was the need to retain and review project management requirements with the entire organization.... Having a validated [project management] system allows us to remain competitive for bidding on those programs that require formal cost schedule control systems.

Kombs Engineering

The company described in the preceding section was very lucky to have identified the crisis and taken the time to react appropriately. Some government contractors have not been so fortunate. Consider Michigan-based Kombs Engineering. (The name of this company is disguised at the company's request.)

By June 1993, Kombs Engineering had yearly sales of $25 million. Its business bases consisted of two contracts with the Department of Energy, one for $15 million and the other for $8 million. The other $2 million came from a variety of small jobs worth $15,000 to $50,000 each.

The larger contract with the Department of Energy was a five-year contract for $15 million per year. The contract had been awarded in 1988 and was up for renewal in 1993. The Department of Energy made it clear that although it was pleased with the technical performance of Kombs so far, the law required that the contract be put up for competitive bidding. The company's marketing intelligence indicated that the Department of Energy intended to spend $10 million per year for five years on the follow-on contract, with a tentative award date of October 1993.

On June 21, Kombs received the department's request for proposal. Because the technical requirements of the request were not considered a problem, the company believed it would win the contract on technical merit alone. However, the government agency also required a section in the proposal on how Kombs would manage the project as well as a complete description of how the project management system worked at Kombs.

That was a big problem. The 1988 bid for the original contract required no information on project management. At that time, all projects at Kombs were accomplished through a traditional organizational structure. Only line managers could act as project leaders.

In July 1993, Kombs hired a consultant to train the entire organization in project management. The consultant also worked closely with the proposal team. The proposal was submitted to the Department of Energy during the second week of August. In September 1993, the department submitted a list of questions to Kombs concerning the proposal. Almost all of the questions involved project management. Kombs responded to all of the department's questions.

In October 1993, Kombs received notification that it would not be granted the contract renewal. During a postaward conference, the Department of Engineering stated that it had no "faith" in the Kombs project management system.

This case shows what happens when a subcontractor fails to recognize how smart the customer is in project management. Had Kombs kept in close contact with its customers, it would have had five years instead of one month to develop a believable project management system. Kombs Engineering is no longer in business.

Mason & Hanger Corporation

Some companies have learned the importance of staying close to their customers and the danger of allowing a customer to become more knowledgeable than the company is in project management. Mason & Hanger Corporation has an effective project management system. Asked what allowed the company to accelerate the implementation of effective project management, John "Skip" Drummond, vice president for quality, said:

> Continuing demand by the Department of Energy to "do more with less" caused us to rethink the methods we used to allocate resources to our work. We found ourselves beginning to overcommit resources in many areas, especially in our process engineering and risk management departments. This became especially noticeable in the early 1990s. We believe that our strong project management culture enables us to better "partner" with our customers by doing a better job of aligning our resources with their expectations!

Williams Machine Tool Company

The strength of a corporate culture can often keep a company from recognizing that change is needed. It can also make the implementation of change more difficult. Such is the situation of Williams Machine Tool Company (another disguised case).

For 75 years, the company provided quality products to its clients, by 1980 becoming the third-largest machine-tool company based in the United States. The company was highly profitable, and compensation and benefits were generous. For that reason, it enjoyed an extremely low employee turnover rate.

Between 1970 and 1980, the company's profits reached an unprecedented level. Its success came from one product line of standard machine tools. Williams spent most of its time and effort in looking for ways to improve its bread-and-butter product line, rather than developing new products. The product line was so successful that customers were willing to modify their production lines around Williams's machine tools instead of asking the company to make major modifications to its products.

The company had become extremely complacent by 1980, expecting its phenomenal success with one product line to carry it for 20 or 25 more years. The recession of 1979 through 1983, however, forced its management to rethink. Customers' cutbacks in production decreased the overall demand for standard machine tools. More and more companies were asking for major modification to Williams's standard tools or completely new product designs.

In a changing marketplace, Williams's senior managers recognized that a new strategic focus was called for. Lower-level managers and the general work force, however, put up strong resistance to change. The employees, many of them with more than 20 years of employment at Williams, refused to recognize the need for change. They believed that good times would return after the recession.

In 1986, the company was sold to Crock Engineering (another pseudonym). The red ink continued to flow for Williams, and Crock decided to replace all the Williams senior managers with its own personnel. Crock also announced that it intended to become a specialty machine-tool manufacturer. The company made it clear that employees who could not support this new direction would be replaced. The quarter ending March 31, 1992, was its first profitable quarter in over six years.

After almost 85 years in business, the Williams division was sold again, and 80 percent of its employees lost their jobs. Williams Machine Tool Company did not realize until it was too late that it needed to change its business base from one that was production driven to one that was project driven. For businesses to survive, especially in highly competitive environments, they must look ahead aggressively and recognize that change is inevitable.

Other Driving Forces

Not all companies are driven by one single force. One paint manufacturer, Sherwin-Williams Company, can point to four driving forces behind its implementation of project management.

* Rapid growth through acquisitions
* Emphasis on new product development
* Emphasis on ability to measure the effectiveness of research and development
* Use of the ISO 9000 certification program

ISO 9000 is an internationally recognized quality system standard applicable to any product, service, or process anywhere in the world. ISO 9000 is a three-part, never-ending cycle, including planning, controlling, and documentation.

There are other driving forces that are usually not as pronounced as the seven discussed in this chapter. Some of the additional driving forces include the need for better internal control, the need for better planning, the need to meet a customer's technical requirements, or simply the need to do what the competitors are doing.

Project Management Systems and Tools

Creating a workable system for project management is no easy task. One of the biggest mistakes made is developing a different system for each type of project. Another is failing to integrate the project management system and project management tools into a single process. When companies develop project management systems and tools in tandem, two benefits emerge. First, the work is accomplished with fewer scope changes. And, second, the processes are designed to create minimal disturbance to ongoing business operations.

This chapter discusses the components of system development and some of the most widely used project management tools. Three detailed examples of systems at work are also included.

Critical Components of System Development

Simply having a project management system and following it does not lead to success and excellence in project management. The need for improvements in the system may be critical. External factors can have a strong influence on the success or failure of a company's project management system. Change is a given in the current business climate, and there's no sign that the future will be any different. The rapid changes in technology that have driven changes in project management over the past two decades are not likely to subside. Another trend, the increasing sophistication of consumers and clients, is likely to continue, not go away. Cost and quality control have become virtually the same issue in many industries. Other external factors include rapid mergers and acquisitions, and real-time communications.

Project management systems need to change as the organization changes in response to the ever-evolving business climate. But such changes require that managers on all levels be committed to the changes and develop a vision that calls for the development of project management systems along with the rest of their organizations.

Developing a standard project management system is not for every company. For companies with small or short-term projects, such formal systems may not be cost-effective or appropriate. However, for companies with large or ongoing projects, developing a workable project management system is mandatory.

Let's look at an example. A company that manufactures home fixtures had several project development protocols in place. When they decided to begin using project management systematically, the complexity of the company's current methods became apparent. The company had multiple systems development methodologies based on the type of project. This became awkward for employees who had to struggle with a different methodology for each project. The company then opted to create a general, all-purpose methodology for all projects. The new methodology had flexibility built into it. According to one spokesman for the company:

> Our project management approach, by design, is not linked to a specific systems development methodology. Because we believe that it is better to use a [standard] systems development methodology than to decide which one to use, we have begun development of a *guideline* systems development methodology specific for our organization. We have now developed *prerequisites* for project success. These include: well-patterned methodology, clear set of objectives, well-understood expectations, and thorough problem definition.

> The moral here: Don't reinvent the wheel. But don't develop a system from scratch, either.

The critical components of project management system development are organization, management, and reporting.

Organizing the Project

Every project begins with an idea, a vision for the future, or a business opportunity that is tied to the organization's overall business objectives. The next step in organizing the project is setting goals and then deciding how the goals are going to be accomplished.

Then, the project charter is drawn up. It serves as the foundation of the project. It defines the contract and the parties involved. And the charter includes the following:

- A statement of business needs
- An agreement on what the project will deliver
- An identification of project dependencies
- A description of the roles and responsibilities of project team members
- A list of standards for setting the project budget

Once the project charter has been defined, a period of research and information finding begins. Enough solid information must be gathered to support the project's goals and objectives, to assess the risk involved in the project, and to minimize potential problems that might come up later. This stage of project planning should generate enough information to clearly establish project deliverables and outline the resources that will be needed to complete the project. The deliverables are critical. The accomplishment of each one will affect how well the project meets its goals, whether it stays on schedule and on budget, and ultimately the quality of the finished product.

Every phase of the project organization process should include planned review points. It is vital that the reviewers for the project be identified as early as possible. A balance between the two types of reviewers—content experts and managers—is an important consideration.

Managing the Project

The project manager and the project team are charged with the everyday management and control of the project as it operates. They evaluate the project's progress, assess the project's performance, and control the development of deliverables. As the project proceeds, the following activities go on continuously:

- Evaluation of the daily progress made on tasks and deliverables as measured by meeting budgets, quality standards, and schedules
- Adjustment of day-to-day project assignments and deliverables in reaction to immediate variances, issues, and problems
- Proactive resolution of project issues and implementation of changes to control scope creep
- Assessment of client's level of satisfaction
- Periodic and structured reviews of deliverables
- Centralized maintenance of project control files

Reporting the Results

Status reporting keeps the project on course and in good health. Status reports should contain the following information:

- Major accomplishments to date
- Planned accomplishment for the next period
- Project progress summary that includes the following elements:
  —Percentage of effort hours consumed
  —Percentage of budget costs consumed
  — Percentage of project schedule consumed
- Project cost summary (budget versus actual)
- Project issues and concerns
- Quality issues
- Management action items

The last three elements of the project status report provide information on issues and concerns that may affect the progress of the project. If issues and concerns are managed and reported as they come up, the momentum of the project can be protected at the same time some flexibility in handling problems can be maintained. Issues and concerns about the project are areas that require action from the project manager, the project team, the project sponsor, or the company's executive managers. Decisions made on project issues must be clearly defined and communicated to the project team. This ensures an appropriate level of tracking and monitoring. This same principle pertains to the management of changes in scope, which come up inevitably in most projects. Managing scope change means managing the potential effects on budget, schedule, and deliverables. The effects of changes in the main project should also be monitored for their potential impact on related projects.

Systems Development at Work

Let's consider some examples of systems and tools at work in three companies: Key Services Corporation, General Motors Powertrain Group, and Ericsson Telecom AB.

Key Services Corporation

Merger mania hit the U.S. banking community during the late 1980s. The result was a lowering of costs owing to economies of scale and increased competition. The banking community recognized the importance of using project management techniques for mergers and acquisitions. The faster the cultures of newly merged or acquired banking organizations could be combined, the less impact on an organization's bottom line.

Key Services Corporation is an excellent example of how to leverage a project management system as a framework for project development and implementation. Key is one of the nation's largest financial services organizations, with assets of approximately $67 billion. Most of Key's projects (90 percent) are internal, and its business includes project-driven as well as non-project-driven activities. The budgets for Key's projects range from $5,000 to $16 million. Through its three principal lines of business (corporate banking, consumer finance, and community banking), Cleveland-based Key Services Corporation provides retail and wholesale banking, investment, financing, and money management services to individuals and organizations across the nation, in 44 states from Maine to Alaska.

To determine the weaknesses associated with past management systems, the information systems reengineering team conducted focus groups with project management staff. The focus groups pointed out the following problems:

- Lack of management commitment
- Lack of a feedback mechanism for project managers to determine the updates and revisions needed in the system

- Lack of adaptable methods for the organization
- Lack of a training program for project managers
- Lack of focus on consistent and periodic communication on the progress of system deployment
- Lack of focus on project management tools and techniques

On the basis of this feedback, the team successfully developed and deployed a project management and system development methodology. Over the period from June to December of 1996, the target audience of 300 project managers became aware and then applied a project management system and standard tool (Microsoft Project). They continue to do so. According to Diane Wohlleber, a member of the information systems reengineering team:

> The success of this methodology and tool deployment is attributed to a strong management commitment, structured training curriculum, solid support team infrastructure, centralized Lotus Notes Repository where methodology is housed and controlled, and periodic communication updates. As with any methodology, there is a large marketing component associated with ensuring the success.

One of Key's goals in implementing project management was to introduce new products and services more quickly. Another was to cut the time required to complete mergers and acquisitions and assimilate the acquired organizations into the corporation. Key also wanted to be able to manage all of its projects better.

The successful development of the project management system at Key was based on the involvement of employees. Training in project management principles was provided, and project management was acknowledged as a profession. Employees were encouraged to sit for the project management certification examination.

Key Services College is the training arm of Key Services Corporation. The college has been instrumental in the success of project management at Key. According to Peggy Farinacci, vice president of the college, "through partnerships with both the technology services group and the operations services group," Key Services College was "successful in assisting each division in developing a common, shared, project management strategy." The college "brought these groups together to agree on a standard methodology and tool. Then we facilitated the development of a curriculum to help new and existing project managers learn and apply the methodology and tool." As a result of the development of a standard project management system, Key also has created a project management manual for mergers and acquisitions.

Simply having a project management system and using it does not lead to excellence in project management. A need for improving the system must exist. Phillip Carter, vice president of Key Services Corporation, identified the driving forces that pressured his company to strive for success:

> … [The] rapid change in technology and consumer expectations and the increased focus on quality and cost control [were the driving forces]. Banking has been and continues to be in a state of rapid change. Mergers and advancement of technology have forced [companies in] the banking industry to change or fail or be acquired.

Project management systems can change as the organization changes. However, management must be committed to the change and have the vision to let project management systems evolve with the organization.

Key Services Corporation did an outstanding job of creating a system that reflects guidelines rather than inflexible policies and procedures. The system can be used for projects in both technology and business, and it has been shown that project management can be used to improve product quality and shorten project schedules. Because employees are being trained to use the system consistently, Key Services Corporation is building a culture that uses project management to satisfy customers with quality products and faster services and to generate cost savings. As Gary Didier, executive vice president of Key Services Corporation's continuous improvement group, said:

> Today, most companies are focused on quality improvement to achieve customer satisfaction. At Key Services, we're using project management as a strategic tool that will enable us to deliver quality *faster* than ever before. We've deployed a standard set of project management tools and techniques that help us drive the competi-

tive advantage by increasing the speed at which we deliver world class results.

General Motors Powertrain Group

General Motors Powertrain Group is another example of a large company achieving excellence in project management. The company's business is based primarily on internal projects, although some contract projects are taken on for external customers. The size of the group's projects ranges from $100 million to $1.5 billion. Based in Pontiac, Michigan, the GM Powertrain Group has developed and implemented a four-phase project management system that has become the core process for its business. The company decided to go to project management in order to get its products out to the market faster. According to Michael Mutchler, vice president and group executive, "The primary expectation I have from a product-focused organization is effective execution. This comprehends disciplined and effective product program development, implementation, and day-to-day operations." He continued:

> Project teams were formed to create an environment in which leaders could gain a better understanding of market and customer needs; to foster systems thinking and cross-functional, interdependent behavior and to enable all employees to understand their role in executing GM Powertrain strategies and delivering outstanding products. This organization's strategy is aimed at enabling a large organization to be responsive and to deliver quality products that customers want and can afford.

The project management system at GM Powertrain is documented and based on common templates, checklists, and processes. The following elements are common across all GM Powertrain projects.

- A project team organizational structure that includes defined roles and responsibilities
- Project plans, schedules, and logic networks
- Project-level and part-level tracking systems
- A four-phase product development process
- An organized change management process

- A part readiness process
- A project charter and contract

One of the signs of a well-managed organization is the ability to perform strategic planning for continuous improvement in the project management system. GM Powertrain has demonstrated this ability well. (See Table 4-1.) Two other critical elements of GM Powertrain's project management system are its charter and contract features. The project charter is issued to newly appointed project teams. It defines the scope of the project through measurable objectives, including:

- Business purpose
- Strategic objectives
- Results sought
- Engineering and capital budget
- Project schedule

Table 4-1.   GM Powertrain's strategic plan for continuous improvement in its project management system.

Current System	Future System
Timing plans	Integrated logic networks
Different procedures for each project or project team	Standard procedures across projects
Multiple scheduling tools	Standard scheduling tools
Reworking due to lack of templates	Standard templates
Inconsistent reporting content and format	Standard reporting across the project teams

The project contract specifies how the project will fulfill the project charter. Prepared by the project team, the contract documents a shared understanding of what the team will deliver and what the rest of the GM Powertrain staff will provide in terms of resources and support to the team. The contract:

- Clarifies the portfolio product assignment as defined by the charter
- Defines the boundaries of the project

- Identifies the resources, economics, materials, schedules, and processes needed to fulfill the charter successfully
- Is signed by the functional managers involved to clearly demonstrate their belief that the project can be implemented successfully
- Provides a system for required renegotiation of contract terms when unforeseen factors have an adverse impact on the project's likelihood of fulfilling its charter

The General Motors Powertrain Group has achieved its goal of getting products to market faster. But it has also learned some lessons along the way. The group now knows that its project management system needs to be continuously improved. For example, it knows that there's still a need to reduce variations in the project management processes to achieve a more standardized system.

Ericsson Telecom AB

Key Services Corporation and General Motors Powertrain are examples of project management systems designed for internal customers. Ericsson Telecom AB's challenges are more complex. Most of Ericsson's projects (80 percent) are undertaken on behalf of external clients, and so its business is mostly project driven.

Ericsson Telecom AB is a large, international telecommunications corporation with headquarters in Stockholm, Sweden. In this discussion, we will be looking at the company's Dallas, Texas, operations. Ericsson's projects range in size from $100,000 to $1 billion.

In 1989, Ericsson developed a project management system it called PROPS. Initially designed for use at Business Area Public Telecommunications for technical development projects, the system has been applied throughout the 130 countries in which Ericsson does business. It has been used successfully with all kinds of projects.

New users and different fields of application have increased the demands on PROPS. Users provide feedback on the lessons learned on their projects so that PROPS can be kept up-to-date. In 1994, a second generation of PROPS was developed to include applications for small projects, concurrent engineering projects, and cross-functional projects. Increasing project quality was a primary focus in the 1994 revision.

The 1994 version of PROPS is generic in nature and can be used in all types of organizations. The success of PROPS worldwide proves that rigid policies and procedures are not needed to achieve excellence in project management. PROPS can be used in all types of projects, including product development, organizational development, construction, and marketing. It has been applied successfully in large, small, and cross-functional projects. PROPS focuses on every aspect of business operations, from customer satisfaction to profitability to effective resource applications.

Ericsson's project management system is based on tollgates and project sponsorship. This ensures that projects are initiated and procured in a business-oriented manner and that the benefits for the customer, as well as for Ericsson, are fully considered before a project is taken to contract.

The PROPS system is completely generic. As such, it is flexible and can be applied to many different kinds of projects, internal and external. The cornerstones of this generic project system are these:

- Tollgates
- Project models
- Work models
- Milestones

Tollgates are superordinate decision points in the project. Formal decisions are made at each tollgate concerning the goals and execution of the project. The tollgate concept is applied throughout Ericsson worldwide. In PROPS, five tollgates constitute the backbone of the system. The function and position of the tollgates are standardized for all types of projects.

The project sponsor makes the tollgate decisions and takes overall business responsibility for the entire project as well as its outcomes. The tollgate decision procedure includes project assessment and preparation of an executive summary that gives the project sponsor a basis for making a decision. The project and its outcomes are evaluated from several different perspectives: the project's status, consumption of resources, and expected benefits to the customer and to Ericsson. The following decisions are made at the five tollgates:

- Decision on start-of-project feasibility study
- Decision on execution of the project
- Decision on continued execution, confirmation of the project, or revision of its limits, and implementation of design

- Decision on use of the final project results, handover to customer, limited introduction to the market
- Decision on project conclusion

The project model describes which project management activities are to be performed and which project documents are to be prepared. The project model is broken down into four phases: prestudy, feasibility study, execution, and conclusion. The project sponsor initiates the project and makes tollgate decisions. Most of the other activities in the project model are the responsibility of the project manager.

The prestudy phase assesses feasibility from the technical and commercial viewpoints based on the expressed and unexpressed requirements and needs of external and internal customers. During the prestudy phase, a set of alternative solutions is formulated. A rough estimate is made of the schedule and amount of work needed for the project's implementation alternatives.

The feasibility study phase forms a secure basis for the future project and prepares for the successful execution of the project. As part of the feasibility study, various realization alternatives and their potential consequences are analyzed, as well as their potential to fulfill the customers' requirements. At this point, the project goals and strategies are defined, project plans are prepared, and potential risks are assessed. Contract negotiations are initiated, and project organization is defined comprehensively.

During the execution phase of the project model, the project is carried through as planned with respect to schedule, budget, and accomplishments. The goal of this phase is to fully attain the project's original goals and meet or surpass the customers' requirements. Technical work is executed by the line organization according to processes and working methods defined earlier in the project. Project work is actively controlled. This means that the project's progress is continuously checked and that action is taken when necessary to keep the project on track.

The conclusion phase discontinues the project's operation, compiles a record of the lessons learned, and ensures that every outstanding matter has been addressed. During this phase, the resources placed at the project manager's disposal are discontinued. In addition, the project manager and sponsor suggest measures to improve the project model, the work model, and the project management processes for future applications.

The work model describes the activities to be performed in order to achieve each specific result planned for the project. To arrive at a complete description for a specific project, one or more work models need to be defined and linked to the general project model. A work model combined with the general project model is a PROPS application. If there are no suitable work models described for a project, it is the project manager's responsibility to define activities and milestones so that the project plan can be followed and the project actively controlled.

Milestones are also defined as part of the work model. A milestone is an intermediate objective that defines an important, measurable event in the project's life and represents a result that must be achieved at a specified point. Milestones link the work models to the project model. Clearly defined milestones are essential for monitoring progress, especially in large and/or long-term projects. In addition to providing a way to structure the time schedule, milestones not achieved indicate potential project delays. Milestones also help make the project's progress visible to the project team and the project sponsor. Before each milestone is reached, a milestone review is performed to check the results achieved against preset criteria. The project manager is responsible for the milestone review.

Ericsson's worldwide success can be partially attributed to the acceptance and consistent use of the PROPS model. Ericsson has demonstrated that success can be achieved with even the simplest of models and without rigid policies and procedures.

Project Management Tools

As little as five years ago, many of the companies described in this book had virtually no project management capabilities. How did these companies implement project management so fast? The answer came with the explosion of personal computer-based software for project planning, estimating, and scheduling.

Until the late 1980s, the project management tools in use were software packages designed for project scheduling. The most prominent were:

• Program Evaluation and Review Technique (PERT)

- Arrow Diagramming Method (ADM)
- Precedence Diagramming Method (PDM)

These three networking and scheduling techniques provided project managers with computer capabilities that far surpassed the bar charts and milestone charts that had been in use. The three software programs proved invaluable at the time.

- They formed the basis for all planning and predicting and provided management with the ability to plan for the best possible use of resources to achieve a given goal within schedule and budget constraints.
- They provided visibility and enabled management to control one-of-a-kind programs.
- They helped management handle the uncertainties involved in programs by answering such questions as how time delays influence project completion, where slack exists among elements, and which elements are crucial to meeting the completion date. This feature gave managers a means for evaluating alternatives.
- They provided a basis for obtaining the necessary facts for decision making.
- They utilized a so-called time network analysis as the basic method of determining manpower, material, and capital requirements as well as providing a means for checking progress.
- They provided the basic structure for reporting information.

Unfortunately, scheduling techniques can't replace planning. And scheduling techniques are only as good as the quality of the information that goes into the plan. Criticisms of the three scheduling techniques in the 1970s included the following:

- Time, labor, and intensive effort were required to use them.
- The ability of upper-level management to contribute to decision making may have been reduced.
- Functional ownership of the estimates was reduced.
- Historical data for estimating time and cost were lost.
- The assumption of unlimited resources was inappropriate.
- The amount of detail required made full use of the scheduling tools inappropriate.

Advancements in the memory capabilities of mainframe computer systems during the 1990s eventually made it possible to overcome many of the deficiencies in the three scheduling techniques being used in project management in the 1970s and 1980s. There emerged an abundance of mainframe software that combined scheduling techniques with both planning and estimating capabilities. Estimating then could include historical databases, which were stored in the mainframe memory files. Computer programs also proved useful in resource allocation. The lessons learned from previous projects could also be stored in historical files. This improved future planning as well as estimating processes.

The drawback was that mainframe project management software packages were very expensive and user-unfriendly. The mainframe packages were deemed more appropriate for large projects in aerospace, defense, and large construction. For small- and medium-size companies, the benefits did not warrant the investment.

The effective use of project management software of any kind requires that project teams and managers first understand the principles of project management. All too often, an organization might purchase a mainframe package without training its employees how to use it in the context of project management.

For example, in 1986, a large, nationally recognized hospital purchased a $130,000 mainframe software package. The employees in the hospital's information systems department were told to use the package for planning and reporting the status of all projects. Less than 10 percent of the organization's employees were given any training in project management. Training people in the use of software without first training them in project management principles proved disastrous. The morale of the organization hit an all-time low point, and eventually no one even used the expensive software.

Generally speaking, mainframe software packages are more difficult to implement and use than smaller personal computer–based packages. The reason? Mainframe packages require that everyone use the same package, often in the same way. A postmortem study conducted at the hospital identified the following common difficulties during the implementation of its mainframe package.

- Upper-level managers sometimes didn't like the reality of the results.
- Upper-level managers did not use the packages for planning, budgeting, and decision making.

- Day-to-day project planners sometimes didn't use the packages for their own projects.
- Some upper-level managers sometimes didn't demonstrate support and commitment to training.
- Use of the mainframe software required a strong internal communications line for support.
- Clear, concise reports were lacking.
- Mainframe packages didn't always provide for immediate turnaround of information.
- The hospital had no project management standards in place prior to the implementation of the new software.
- Implementation highlighted the inexperience of some middle managers in project planning and in applying organizational skills.
- Neither the business environment nor the organization's structure supported the hospital's project management/planning needs.
- Sufficient/extensive resources (staff, equipment, etc.) were required.
- The business entity didn't determine the extent of, and appropriate use of, the systems within the organization.
- The system was viewed by some employees as a substitute for the extensive interpersonal skills required of the project manager.
- Software implementation didn't succeed because the hospital's employees didn't have sufficient training in project management principles.

Today, project managers have a large array of personal computer-based software available for planning, scheduling, and controlling projects. Packages such as Microsoft Project have almost the same capabilities as mainframe packages. Microsoft Project can import data from other programs for planning and estimating and then facilitate the difficult tasks of tracking and controlling multiple projects.

The simplicity of personal computer–based packages and their user-friendliness has been especially valuable in small- and medium-size companies. The packages are so affordable that even the smallest of companies can master project management and adopt a goal of reaching project management excellence.

Clearly, even the most sophisticated software package can never be a substitute for competent project leadership. By itself such packages can't identify or correct task-related problems. But they can be terrific tools for the project manager to use in tracking the many interrelated variables and tasks that come into play in contemporary project management. Specific examples of such capabilities include the following:

- Project data summary: expenditure, timing, and activity data
- Project management and business graphics capabilities
- Data management and reporting capabilities
- Critical path analyses
- Customized as well as standardized reporting formats
- Multiproject tracking
- Subnetworking
- Impact analysis
- Early-warning systems
- Online analyses of recovering alternatives
- Graphical presentations of cost, time, and activity data
- Resource planning and analyses
- Cost and variance analyses
- Multiple calendars
- Resource leveling

Planning for Excellence

Planning for excellence in project management needs to consider all aspects of the company: from the working relationships among employees and managers and between staff and management, to the roles of the various players (especially the role of executive project sponsors), to the company's corporate structure and culture. Other aspects of project management must also be planned. Strategic planning is vital for every company's health. Effective project planning can mean the difference between success and failure. Even career planning for individual project managers ultimately plays a part in a company's excellence in project management or its mediocrity. All of these subjects are discussed in this chapter.

Influence of Economic Conditions

During favorable economic times, changes in management style and corporate culture move very slowly. But favorable economic conditions don't last forever. The period between recognizing the need for change and garnering the ability to manage change is usually measured in years. As economic conditions deteriorate, change occurs more and more quickly in business organizations, but not fast enough to keep up with the economy.

Before the recession of 1989–1993, U.S. companies were willing to accept the implementation of project management at a tedious pace. Corporate managers in general believed that their guidance was sufficient to keep their companies healthy, and outside consultants were brought in primarily to train production workers in the principles of project management. Executive training sessions, even very short ones, were rarely offered.

During the recession, senior managers came to realize that their knowledge of project management was not as comprehensive as they had once believed. (See Table 5-1.) It shows how the recession affected the development of project management systems.

Table 5-1.   Effects of the 1989–1993 recession on the implementation of project management.

Factor	Before the Recession	After the Recession
Strategic focus	Short-term	Long-term
Organizational structuring	To secure power, authority, and control	To get closer to customers
Management focus	To manage people	To manage work and deliverables
Sponsorship	Lip service	Active
Training emphasis	Quantitative	Qualitative/behavioral
Risk analysis	Minimal effort	Concerted effort
Authority	In writing	Implied
Team building	Functional teams	Cross-functional teams

To address the far-reaching changes in the economic environment, senior managers began to ask a fundamental question: How do we plan for excellence in project management? In answering this question, it would be futile to expect managers to implement immediately all of the changes needed to set up modern project management in their companies. (The principles of modern project management are discussed in Chapter 6.) What senior managers needed was a plan like the one shown in Table 5-2, expressed in terms of three broad critical success factors: qualitative factors, organizational factors, and quantitative factors.

Table 5-2.   Factors in achieving excellence.

Factor	Short-Term Applications	Long-Term Implications
Qualitative	Provide educational training	Emphasize cross-functional working relationships and team building
	Dispel illusion of a need for authority	
	Share accountability	
	Commit to estimates and deliverables	
	Provide visible executive support and sponsorship	
Organizational	Deemphasize policies and procedures	Create project management career path
	Emphasize guidelines	Provide project managers with reward/penalty power
	Use project charters	Use nondedicated, cross-functional teams
Quantitative	Use a single tool for planning, scheduling, and controlling	Use estimating databases

Critical Success Factors

Critical success factors include those activities that must be performed if the organization is to achieve its long-term objectives. Most businesses have only a handful of critical success factors. However, if even one of them were not executed successfully, the business's competitive position would be threatened.

The critical success factors in achieving project management excellence apply equally to all types of organizations, even those that have not fully implemented their project management systems. Though most organizations are sincere in their efforts to fully implement their systems, stumbling blocks are inevitable and must be overcome. Here's a list of common complaints from project teams.

- There's scope creep in every project and no way to avoid it.
- Completion dates are set before project scope and requirements have been agreed upon.
- Detailed project plans identifying all of the project's activities, tasks, and subtasks are not available.
- Projects emphasize deadlines. We should emphasize milestones and quality and not time.
- Senior managers don't always allow us to use pure project management techniques. Too many of them are still date driven instead of requirements driven. Original target dates should be used only for broad planning.
- Project management techniques from the 1960s are still being used on most projects. We need to learn how to manage from a plan and how to use shared resources.
- Sometimes we are pressured to cut estimates low to win a contract, but then we have to worry about how we'll accomplish the project's objectives.
- There are times when line personnel not involved in a project change the project budget to maintain their own chargeability. Management does the same.
- Hidden agendas come into play. Instead of concentrating on the project, some people are out to set precedents or score political points.
- We can't run a laboratory without equipment, and equipment maintenance is a problem because there's no funding to pay for the materials and labor.
- Budgets and schedules are not coordinated. Sometimes we have spent money according to the schedule but are left with only a small percentage of the project activities complete.
- Juggling schedules on multiple projects is sometimes almost impossible.
- Sometimes we filter information from reports to management because we fear sending them negative messages.
- There's a lot of caving in on budgets and schedules. Trying to be a good guy all the time is a trap.

With these comments in mind, let's look at the three critical success factors in achieving project management excellence.

Qualitative Factors

If excellence in project management is a continuous stream of successfully completed projects, then our first step should be to define *success.* As discussed in Chapter 2, success in projects has traditionally been defined as achieving the project's objectives within the following constraints:

- Allocated time
- Budgeted cost
- Desired performance at technical or specification level
- Quality standards as defined by customers or users

In experienced organizations, the four preceding parameters have been extended to include the following:

- With minimal or mutually agreed upon scope changes
- Without disturbing the organization's corporate culture or values
- Without disturbing the organization's usual work flow

These last three parameters deserve further comment.

Organizations that eventually achieve excellence are committed to quality and upfront planning so that minimal scope changes are required as the project progresses. Those scope changes that are needed must be approved jointly by both the customer and the contractor. A well-thought-out process for handling scope changes is in place in such organizations. Even in large profit-making, project-driven industries such as aerospace, defense, and large construction, tremendous customer pressure can be expected to curtail any "profitable" scope changes introduced by the contractor.

Most organizations have well-established corporate cultures that have taken years to build. On the other hand, project managers may need to develop their own subcultures for their projects, particularly when the projects will require years to finish. Such temporary project cultures must be developed within the limitations of the larger corporate culture. The project manager should not expect senior officers of the company to allow the project manager free rein.

The same limitations affect organizational work flow. Most project managers working in organizations that are only partially project driven realize that line managers in their organizations are committed to providing continuous support to the company's regular functional work. Satisfying the needs of time-limited projects may only be secondary. Project managers are expected to keep the welfare of their whole companies in mind when they make project decisions.

For companies to reach excellence in project management, executives must learn to define project success in terms of both what is good for the project and what is good for the organization.

Executives can support project managers by reminding them of this two-part responsibility by:

- Encouraging project managers to take on nonproject responsibilities such as administrative activities
- Providing project managers with information on the company's operations and not just information pertaining to their assigned projects
- Supporting meaningful dialogue among project managers
- Asking whether decisions made by project managers are in the best interest of the company as a whole

Organizational Factors

Organizational behavior in project management is a delicate balancing act something like sitting on a bar stool. Bar stools usually come with three legs to keep them standing. So does project management: one is the project manager, one is the line manager, and one is the project sponsor. If one of the legs is lost or unusable, the stool will be very difficult to balance.

Although line managers are the key to successful project management, they will have a lot of trouble performing their functions without effective interplay with the project's manager and corporate sponsor. In unsuccessful projects, the project manager has often been vested with power (authority) over the line managers involved. In more successful projects, project and line managers share authority. The project manager negotiates the line managers' commitment to the project and works through line managers rather than around them. Project managers provide recommendations regarding employee performance. And leadership is centered around the whole project team, not just the project manager.

In successful project management systems, the following equation always holds true:

Accountability = Responsibility + Authority

When project and line managers view each other as equals, they share equally in the management of the project and thus they share equally the authority, responsibility, and accountability for the project's success. Obviously, the sharing of authority makes sharing decision making easier. A few suggestions for executive project sponsors follow.

- Do not increase the authority of the project manager at the expense of the line managers.
- Allow line managers to provide technical direction to their people, if at all possible.
- Encourage line managers to provide realistic time and resource estimates and then work with the line managers to make sure they keep their promises.
- Above all, keep the line managers fully informed.

In organizations that have created effective project management systems, the role of the executive manager has changed along with project management. Early in the implementation of project management, executives were actively involved in the everyday project management process. But as project management has come into its own and general economic conditions have changed, their involvement has become more passive, and they concentrate on long-term and strategic planning. They have learned to trust project managers' decisions and view project management as a central factor in their company's success.

Project sponsors provide visible, ongoing support. Their role is to act as a bodyguard for the project and the project manager. Unlike other executives on the senior management team, individual project sponsors may play a more active role in projects, depending on how far along the project is. Early in the project's functioning, for example, the project sponsor might help the project manager define the project's requirements. Once that is done, the sponsor resumes a less active role and receives project information only as needed.

In successful project management systems that carry a high volume of ongoing project work, an executive sponsor may not be assigned to low-dollar-value or low-priority projects. Middle managers may fill the sponsorship role in some cases. But no matter the size or value of the project, project sponsors today are responsible for the welfare of all members of their project teams and not just the project manager.

The existence of a project sponsor implies visible, ongoing executive support for project management. And executive support motivates project personnel to excel. Executive project sponsorship also supports the development of an organizational culture that fosters confidence in the organization's project management systems.

Sometimes executives do not recognize the value of project sponsorship. This is particularly true of organizations primarily made up of white-collar professionals who hold advanced degrees. Let's look at a company we'll call Garcia Sciences Corporation, a small company headquartered in Tucson, Arizona.

In 1985 Roy Garcia, M.D., retired as vice president of research and development at a small pharmaceutical company. With more than 30 years of experience in research and development, Dr. Garcia was confident in his ability to start his own medical equipment company. By 1995, Garcia Sciences Corporation employed 120 people and generated $65 million per year in revenue. The research and development group had developed a family of new products that were well accepted by the medical community. State-of-the-art manufacturing techniques were producing high-quality, low-cost products.

Financially, Garcia Sciences Corporation was doing well. However, the company was troubled by detrimental cultural issues. Dr. Garcia began having second thoughts about the corporate culture he had created in the late 1980s. Because most of Dr. Garcia's employees held advanced degrees in engineering or science, he had given his professional employees a great deal of freedom to keep them motivated. Dr. Garcia believed strongly that scientists and engineers needed the freedom to be creative. Project sponsorship did not exist, and individual project teams were empowered to set their own objectives for the projects.

Almost every project was carried through to completion, and canceling projects was unacceptable. Status reporting was infrequent, so that executive managers often interfered in projects just to find out what was going on. Ultimately, Dr. Garcia and several senior managers began canceling projects either because the objectives didn't fit with the organization's overall goals or because the marketplace had changed. Team members became extremely unhappy when their projects were canceled before completion. The morale at Garcia Sciences weakened.

Dr. Garcia recognized that being able to see projects through to completion was what motivated project teams and managers. Through the grapevine, he learned that the project teams believed that their projects were being canceled to satisfy the personal whims of management rather than on the basis of sound business decisions.

It's easy for us to see that Dr. Garcia was operating under the mistaken assumption that advanced degrees prepared people to make intelligent business decisions. There are two kinds of intelligence operating in research and development companies: technical intelligence and business intelligence. Garcia's professional employees had the technical knowledge they needed, but they did not understand the business aspects of their projects.

Still, the problem in this case study did not lay with the employees. It lay with the corporation's senior managers. The key issue was the lack of executive project sponsorship. An executive project sponsor familiar with each project from its first stages would have been able to identify both the technical and the business objectives of the project from the beginning.

In addition to being visible, executive support of projects must be continuous. Let's look at another example: US West, a large telecommunications company headquartered in Denver, Colorado. As described by Linda Kretz, formerly a project manager at US West and now president and chief executive officer of 20/20 Solutions in Atlanta, Georgia:

> Project management as a formal process came about by default rather than design at US West. It took several years to build it up and very little time to ultimately do away with it. I was probably the catalyst [for initiating project management at US West], not because I knew anything about it, but because after being titled a project manager I quickly learned that I wasn't managing to do anything but put out fires.... It started in 1984.... I kept a learning

journal for one year on all of the issues that "bit me on the back-side" and soon came to realize that I was reacting with brute force coordination, not proactively managing anything. I personally started to research project management and began studying available literature. I wrote a local manual based on the principles I learned and trained it to my peers in Oregon. The project results in Oregon were far superior to any of the 14 other states in which US West operated. The results captured the attention of headquarters. I was promoted to a second-level manager and charged with establishing a framework for project management for the company....

I had a staff of 10 managers whose responsibilities were to provide project management support and technical training. We accomplished the following:

- Defined core competencies for project management and established a training curriculum for them

- Defined technical and human resource skills and established a methodology for interviewing potential candidates

- Defined the hardware and software requirements and established a 14-state–wide Macintosh network

- Established the Center for Program Management at University College through the University of Denver. This program provides 20 hours [credit] toward a Master of Technology program if [the students were] degreed or [held] a Certificate in Project Management from the University of Denver

- Established documented processes for project management for MIS, product development, internal capital projects and external customer implementations

- Established a documented RFB process, which increased our win rate considerably

- Trained several hundred project specialists and project and program managers with a class designed to test evidence of learning through documentation of a real project throughout its normal cycle

- Established job descriptions and a salary structure

- Provided technical methods and procedures from a project management perspective

- Actively mentored ongoing projects

At this point, everyone wanted to be on the project management bandwagon. Results were exceptional. It was ... 1991. Then downsizing began in earnest. We found ourselves with new leadership. Our original mentors were gone. Reengineering began with an eye toward centralization. The new "henchmen" decided that project management was a "nice to have" but not necessary. In 1992, my staff was disbanded—considered obsolete. Centralization turned out to be a major mistake. As a company, we were back to brute force coordination.

Project management lived on without [executive support for staff], and I became the project implementation manager of all the project managers in Oregon, Washington, Utah, Idaho, and Montana. My job was to manage project managers. I once again convinced the senior team that a formal process was necessary. I became a certified project management professional (PMP) in 1994 and was the only one of my peers to do so. Approximately 78 percent of my team also received their PMPs. My boss and peers did not buy in to the need for certification, but again my team proved to have very impressive results. My peers ultimately came around, but my boss would not support the process and, therefore, would not provide adequate resources for us to do the job well. He ultimately left the business....

By 1997, US West had purchased Continental Cable, and Atlanta found itself with an entirely new management team who didn't understand or see the need for project management. I could continue on but would not be provided with the resources originally promised. I was tired of fighting the battle [and so I] decided to retire. When I left, they once again disbanded the project management process. The project, which was under control when I left, is now in chaos again.

Some lessons learned:

• Corporations must have senior leadership buy-in. This can only happen it you plan brilliantly, present brilliantly, and defend brilliantly.

• No matter what they are talking about, they are talking about money. Always present to those who hold the purse strings and always present how the money spent up-front is going to affect the bottom line.

• Strategic fit must be understood by all and decisions need to be made that support where the corporation wants to be when it grows up.

• The "not invented here" syndrome is alive and well and will remain—live with it and overcome it by planning brilliantly, presenting brilliantly, and defending brilliantly.

• The "good old boy" network is also here to stay for a while. If you are a woman, particularly in the South, you must wait for them to die. In the meantime, persevere, smile, and let them think it was their idea.

- Vertical management will always hinder the process unless roles and responsibilities are well defined and understood so that they can be supported.

- Make the right decisions for the right reasons. Your moral compass will guide you.

- Even though you are singing the same tune, the audience is always changing. Make sure that the senior team continues to understand the difference between reactive brute force coordination and proactive project management, as well as the costs and savings of each.

Visible executive project sponsorship must exist to keep the project manager–line manager interface in balance.

Quantitative Factors

The third factor in achieving excellence in project management is the implementation and acceptance of project management tools. (See the discussion of project management tools in Chapter 4.) Some companies are quick to implement PERT/CPM tools, but many are reluctant to accept other mainframe or personal computer network software for project planning, project cost estimating, project cost control, resource scheduling, project tracking, project audits, or project management information systems.

Mainframe project management tools have been resurrected in the past few years. These new mainframe products are being used mainly for total company project control. However, executives have been slow to accept these sophisticated tools.

Project management education must precede software training. Executives must provide the same encouragement and support for using the new software as the do for project management.

Organizational Restructuring

Effective project management cultures are based on trust, communication, cooperation, and teamwork. When the basis of project management is strong, organizational structure becomes almost irrelevant. (Culture is discussed in detail in Chapter 8.) Restructuring an organization only to add project management is unnecessary and perhaps even dangerous. Companies may need to be restructured for other reasons, such as making the customer more important. But successful project management can live within any structure, no matter how awful the structure looks on paper, just as long as the culture of the company promotes teamwork, cooperation, trust, and effective communication.

The organizations of companies excellent in project management can take almost any form. Today, small- to medium-size companies sometimes restructure to pool management resources. Large companies tend to focus on the strategic business unit as the foundation of their structures. Many companies still follow matrix management. Any can work with project management as long as they have the following traits:

- They are organized around nondedicated project teams.
- They have a flat organizational hierarchy.
- They practice informal project management.
- They do not consider the reporting level of product managers important.

The first point listed above may be somewhat controversial. Dedicated project teams have been a fact of life since the late 1980s. Although there have been many positive results from dedicated teams, there has also been a tremendous waste of manpower coupled with duplication of equipment, facilities, and technologies. Today, most experienced organizations believe that they are scheduling resources effectively so that multiple projects can make use of scarce resources at the same time. And, they believe, nondedicated project teams can be just as creative as dedicated teams, and perhaps at a lower cost.

Although tall organizational structures with multiple layers of management were the rule when project management came on the scene in the early 1960s, today's organizations tend to be lean and mean, with fewer layers of management than ever. The span of control has been widened, and the results of that change have been mass confusion in some companies but complete success in others. The simple fact is that flat organizations work better: They are characterized by better internal communication, cooperation among employees and managers, and atmospheres of trust.

In addition, today's product management organizations, with only a few exceptions (purely product-driven companies), prefer to use informal project management. With formal project management systems, the authority and power of project managers must be documented in writing. Formal project management policies and procedures are required. And documentation is required on the most simple tasks. By contrast, in informal systems, paperwork is minimized. In the future, I believe that even totally project-driven organizations will develop more informal systems.

The reporting level for project managers has fluctuated between top-level and lower-level managers. As a result, some line managers have felt alienated over authority and power disagreements with project managers. In the most successful organizations, the reporting level has stabilized, and project managers and line managers today report at about the same level. Project management simply works better when the managers involved view each other as peers. In large projects, however, project managers may report higher up, sometimes to the executive level. For such projects, a project office is usually set up for project team members at the same level as the line managers with whom they interact daily.

To sum it all up, effective cross-functional communication, cooperation, and trust are bound to generate organizational stability. Let's hope that organizational restructuring on the scale we've seen in recent years will no longer be necessary.

Project Planning

The most critical phase of any project is the planning phase. Ideally, when the project is planned carefully, success is likely. Still, no matter how much or how well we plan, changes are needed and contingencies must be developed.

In the early days of project management, planning was performed from milestone to milestone. This approach led to suboptimization of the individual project segments and resulted in very little regard for the total effort. Today, in successful project management organizations, all projects are broken down into similar life cycle phases. This provides consistency among projects, and it provides checkpoints at which managers can either cancel or redirect individual projects.

Successful project management systems today also include policy and procedure manuals that facilitate consistency among projects. The manuals don't have to be long, sometimes only 20 or 30 pages, and they aren't usually complex. Audit trails are another characteristic common to successful organizations. They make it possible for employees to learn from both their successes and their failures. And finally, they have project managers who are not tempted to micromanage and who rely on the line managers to manage staff at the technical levels of work.

Strategic Planning

Effective strategic planning is necessary to achieve and maintain excellence in project management. In an earlier chapter, we discussed Kombs Engineering and Williams Machine Tool Company. These two companies ultimately went out of business because of poor strategic planning.

One of the best-managed automotive subcontractors in the Detroit area is Standard Products Company in Dearborn, Michigan. When a major automobile producer recently benchmarked automotive subcontractors worldwide, Standard Products was rated the best out of all 19 companies in project management.

Two years ago, Standard Products approached me for assistance in strategic planning, with the goal of maintaining its position of excellence in project management. Its need was simple. For years the automotive subcontractors had been known to handle project management better than the big three automakers in Detroit. Then Ford, Chrysler, and General Motors appeared to be catching up. The questions posed to me by Standard Products were these:

- What will project management look like in the next century?
- What decisions must we make today to ensure that we will maintain our position of excellence into the next century?
- How do we stay ahead of our customers in project management and applications?

Standard Products knew what it had to do. When the customer's project management knowledge surpasses the contractors', the contractor is placed in a dangerous position. Three results are possible, all of them bad for the contractor:

- The customer will want to manage its own projects.
- The customer will dictate to the contractor how to manage the projects.
- The customer will take its business to contractors that have more expertise at project management than it does.

As another case shows, many companies recognize the strategic importance of their project management acumen. During in-house project management training programs, it is usually a good idea to have senior managers make a brief presentation to the participants to show their support for project management. In a previous chapter, we saw how effective this tactic was at Roadway Express. National City Bank of Cleveland, Ohio, has experienced similar success. During a project management training program for National City Bank, the executive vice president for National City Corporation, Jon Gorney, told the class that the excellence of National City's project management systems had allowed the bank to acquire other banks and integrate the acquired banks into National City's culture in less time than other banks allow for mergers and acquisitions. Obviously, National City views project management as an asset that has a very positive effect on the corporate bottom line.

Career Planning

In organizations that successfully manage their projects, project managers are considered professionals and have distinct job descriptions. Employees usually are allowed to climb one of two career ladders: the management ladder or the technical ladder. (They cannot, however, jump back and forth between the two.) This presents a problem to project managers, whose responsibilities bridge the two ladders. To solve this problem, some organizations have created a third ladder, one that fills the gap between technology and management. It is a project management ladder, with the same opportunities for advancement as the other two.

Basics of Modern
Project Management

Sooner or later, all organizations develop some degree of competence in project management. Competence may appear in one functional area such as information systems, in one work group, or in one division of a company. Project management competence may appear in the way an organization performs strategic planning, treats its employees, or reports on the progress of a project.

Some companies need months, some years, and some even decades to achieve even a minimal level of competence. The priority an organization assigns to project management usually determines how quickly changes can occur. Companies go through a number of significant changes as project management is accepted and begins to flourish. Some of us, unfortunately, are so deeply involved that we don't even see the progress that takes place over the weeks and years we devote to it.

Today, projects are being managed a lot differently than they were 40 years ago. Recently, a new approach has taken over the stage: modern project management. The term *modern project management* is used to differentiate what project managers do today from what they did in the past.

This chapter identifies the environmental changes that stimulated the progress in project management practice and explains the 10 components of modern project management. Finally, it explores the implications for achieving excellence in project management over the years to come.

Evolution of Project Management

The history of project management can be broken down into three general periods:

- 1960–1985: Traditional project management
- 1985–1993: Renaissance of project management
- 1993–present: Modern project management

The period of traditional project management was dominated by contractors in the aerospace, defense, and large construction industries. They used project management primarily for very large projects using vast resources. Improving profit levels was definitely the driving force. Assigning dedicated teams to each project was the norm. Cost and schedule took a back seat to the development of technology. And project managers were almost always chosen from the technical ranks.

During this traditional period, companies in other industries were happy to take a wait-and-see attitude while they watched aerospace, defense, and large construction contractors implement project management. Newspaper articles reported on a number of defense and aerospace projects completed years behind schedule and 200 or 300 percent over budget. (The cost overruns and delays were mostly the result of scope changes, but no one mentioned that.) Smaller projects seemed to do much better than large ones. The result of the negative publicity was that project management gained acceptance very slowly over the next two decades.

During what I call the renaissance period for project management, between 1985 and 1993, corporations in various industries finally began to understand that project management could be successfully applied to companies other than large government contractors. It could even improve profitability. Project management was applied to all sizes of projects. And all functional areas of business began to recognize its importance. Multidisciplinary teams became more common, and emphasis was placed on company decisions rather than on project decisions. Personal computer–based project management software gave everyone the opportunity to use sophisticated planning and scheduling tools.

Starting in 1993, companies began recognizing significant changes in the qualitative and organizational areas of project management. These areas were changing so significantly that proponents of project management wanted to differentiate past practices from new, and the term *modern project management* came into use. This change was prompted by the organizations developing some degree of competence in project management. They wanted their clients, employees, and stakeholders to recognize the value of the improvements that had been implemented.

Since 1993, the increasing sophistication of modern tools and techniques has supported projects in all kinds of industries. Project management has spread to virtually all areas of business, no longer confined to organizations that are strictly project driven.

Classification of Companies

From a project management perspective, companies can be classified as project driven, nonproject driven, or a hybrid combination of project and product driven. In project-driven industries such as aerospace, profitability predominantly results from projects successfully completed. In these industries, modern project management is reasonably advanced. In nonproject driven industries, where profitability is measured through the success of functional product lines, progress in modern project management has been slow.

In nonproject-driven companies, projects generally exist to support product lines or general business practices. In such companies, some divisions (for example, management information systems or research and development) are project driven, while most of the business is still based in product lines. We'll refer to these types of companies as hybrids. Gaining the acceptance of modern project management in individual divisions or units where project management and systems development can be combined is relatively easy. But getting it accepted throughout a hybrid organization can be much more difficult.

Surprisingly, during the renaissance period, it was the hybrids that first began accepting the use of project management. Before that, there had been very little support for project management in hybrid companies. Once the benefits of project management became apparent, many hybrids actually started acting like project-driven companies. (See Table 6-1.)

Table 6-1.   Classification of companies by project management utilization.

Project Driven	Hybrid	Nonproject Driven
PM has P&L responsibility	Primarily product driven but with many projects	Very few projects
PM is recognized professional	Emphasis on new product development	Profitability from production
PM has multiple ⟨PRESENT⟩ career paths	Marketing oriented ⟨PAST⟩	Large brick walls
Income comes from projects	Short product life cycles	Long product life cycles
	Rapid development process	
Project Management	Program Management	Product Management

The factor that allowed project management to be accepted so quickly in these companies was the project manager's level of responsibility. In project-driven organizations, profit-and-loss responsibility is tangible and clear-cut. In nonproject-driven companies, profit-and-loss responsibility is a fuzzy area.

Recently, executives in nonproject-driven companies have solved this problem by replacing profit-and-loss statements with cost–benefit analyses. Project managers are frequently asked to update cost–benefit analyses as a condition of continued management support. Project managers maintain a minimum benefit-to-cost ratio or risk having their projects terminated.

Effects of Economic Recession

Economic recessions bring suffering. Downsizings, layoffs, salary and benefit reductions, and plant closings affect employees on every level. But recessions can also be beneficial. Companies are forced to take a long, hard look at the way they do business. If they survive, they'll emerge as more efficient and productive competitors in their markets.

Managers are compelled to make risky decisions during periods of recession. A lot can be learned from the successes and failures that result from risky decisions. It's an unfortunate fact that very few companies document the lessons they learn during hard times.

The recession of 1989–1993 was different from the previous recession of 1979–1983. During the earlier recession, companies emphasized cost cutting, short-term planning, layoffs among blue-collar workers, and the elimination or reduction of funding for training and research and development. Basically, management focused on short-term solutions during the 1979–1983 recession.

Despite numerous success stories, many companies still refused to accept project management as a strategy during recessionary times. Project management continued to be seen as a process that requires a slow, long-term implementation process. It was assumed that changing to project management would constitute culture shock and that business would be disrupted rather than streamlined. Managers during the 1979–1983 recession favored short-term solutions and refused to recognize the benefits of project management. Then, when the recession finally ended, management felt no further pressure to reconsider adopting project management principles. After all, hadn't their companies survived the recession without project management?

Table 6-2 compares the characteristics of the two recent recessions. During the recession of 1989–1993, deep cuts were made among white-collar employees. Layers of management were systematically eliminated, especially middle managers. And companies started focusing on long-term strategic planning. But this most recent recession resulted in lessons learned. Project management today affects every facet of business.

Table 6-2.   Characteristics of recent recessions

Characteristics	1979–1983	1989–1993
Layoffs	Blue collar	White collar
Research and development	Eliminated	Focused
Training	Eliminated	Focused

Table 6-2.   (continued)

Characteristics	1979–1983	1989–1993
Solutions	Short-term	Long-term
Results	Return to status quo	Changed way of doing business
	No support for project management	Risk management
	No allies for project management	Lessons learned documented

Effects of Global Pressures

During the early 1990s, as the most recent recession continued, global pressures for drastically improved quality and shortened product development time became apparent. There was widespread development of widely accepted management concepts such as total quality management, life cycle costing, reengineering, self-directed work teams, and empowerment. As these concepts came on the scene one by one, they brought with them the need for long-term planning:

- 1985: Total quality management
- 1990: Concurrent engineering
- 1991: Empowerment
- 1992: Self-directed work teams
- 1993: Reengineering
- 1994: Life cycle costing

(See Chapter 7 for a discussion of these and other management processes.)

Large computer companies, including IBM, Digital Equipment, and Unisys, reduced their labor forces by over 300,000 people, the majority from white-collar positions. The battering of stock prices and the competitive nature of the computer industry emphasized the need for long-term planning for the decades ahead, not just for a few years ahead. Executives took another look at project management. They saw that it had merit for improving an organization's current financial health as well as ensuring its future.

We can't be certain whether the recession by itself supported the acceptance of project management or whether total quality management and concurrent engineering played a significant role. Even before the recession began in 1989, Johnson Controls had embarked on an aggressive total quality management program that involved all of its employees. By 1987, Johnson Controls had recognized that a marriage between project management and total quality management was possible and that project management could make the implementation of total quality management smoother. When the recession deepened, more and more companies, like Johnson Controls, began to accept the relationship, which accelerated the widespread acceptance of project management.

Changes in the Definition of *Success*

Our definition of success has also changed over the years. During the traditional project management period, success was defined in technical terms only. Did the product work or didn't it? During the renaissance period, time, cost, and performance (at appropriate technical and quality levels) were the main considerations. And for the current modern project management period, time, cost, performance, *and* acceptance by the customer are the primary factors in achieving success. After all, the customer, not the contractor, defines what *quality* is.

For the future, emphasis is being placed on two additional criteria for success: (1) with minimal scope change and (2) without disturbing the ongoing business of the company. The first criterion emphasizes effective project planning. The second stresses the need for making decisions based on what's beneficial for the company as a whole and not just for individual projects.

Velocity of Change

The lesson from the last two recessions comes down to this: If change is necessary, make it as quickly as possible. Procrastination only makes the situation worse. The decision to adopt project management may be made quickly, though the implementation can take years. (See Table 6-3.)

Table 6-3.   The velocity of change for project management implementation.

Traditional Project Management	Renaissance Period	Modern Project Management
Minimum 3 to 5 years	Minimum 3 to 5 years	Minimum 6 to 24 months
Organizational restructuring mandatory	Organizational restructuring mandatory	Restructuring unnecessary
Emphasis on power and authority	Emphasis on power and authority	Emphasis on multifunctional teamwork
Sponsorship not critical	Sponsorship needed	Sponsorship mandatory

Recall the case of Roadway Express discussed in Chapter 3. It is typical of the problems and delays that result from trying to take baby steps toward large-scale change.

Ten Components of Modern Project Management

The ten components of modern project management are:

- Proactive management style
- Teamwork and minimal job descriptions
- Shared accountability
- Shared evaluation of team members
- Business, technical, *and* process skills
- Education and training
- Project planning emphasized
- Project objectives in business terms
- Multilevel project sponsorship
- Project failures due to behavioral factors

Let's discuss them one by one.

Proactive Management Style

Before modern project management, the predominant management style was reactive. There was never enough money to do the initial planning right, but there was always plenty of money to redo the plan two or three more times later. Today, the predominant management style is proactive. When team members bring problems out in the open, project and executive managers will help find solutions. When team members bury problems, they are putting their jobs in jeopardy.

Two factors fostered the change to proactive management. First, project management advocates proactive management through effective initial planning as well as contingency planning. Second, risk management is now an important aspect of corporate decision making.

Teamwork and Minimal Job Descriptions

The authority granted to project managers has varied dramatically. Earlier phases of project management were characterized by very formal authority and defined job descriptions, and later by minimal job descriptions and obvious conflicts over power and authority. Today, teamwork and cooperation are paramount, and project charters and letters of appointment clarify who holds what responsibilities. Ultimate responsibility rests with the executive project sponsor, who delegates authority according to the project charter. In most companies excellent in project management, job descriptions have disappeared or only contain explanations of duties and responsibilities with no mention of authority levels.

Shared Accountability

During the first years of project management, the best technical experts were assigned as project managers. They negotiated with line managers to secure the resources needed to complete each project. Each project manager was solely accountable for the success or failure of his or her project by virtue of his or her technical knowledge. Over the years, accountability has been extended to members of the project team. This forced project managers to become more aggressive in recruiting qualified people for their teams. The result? The relationship between project managers and line managers became hostile and competitive.

Today, accountability is shared equally between the line manager and the project manager. And project managers must negotiate with other line and project managers to secure the resources and deliverables they need. Line managers must be accountable for fulfilling the project commitments they make at the same time they provide daily supervision of technical workers assigned to the projects.

Shared Evaluation of Team Members

When the structure of an organization changes or when the organization adopts some form of project management that mandates multiple reporting relationships, the first concern of the employees is the wage and salary program. Typical questions include:

- Will I be paid more or less?
- Will I report higher or lower on the management ladder?
- Who will evaluate my performance for salary increases and promotions?
- How much input will the project manager have on my performance review?
- Is the project manager qualified to evaluate me and, if so, in what areas?
- How will my immediate superior know how well or how poorly I performed on the project?

Organizations can never implement change until they are prepared to revise their wage and salary administration programs.

Over the past 35 years, companies using project management systems have changed the way they evaluate the members of project teams. The central object of these changes has been the role of the project manager. Initially, the project manager provided no input. Later, informal input was allowed in many companies. Again, the problem was the position of project managers in the overall corporate structure. Employees found it difficult to accept that their salary reviews were being handled by a nonexecutive manager who might be two or three job grades below them. Today, this problem has been addressed. Most project managers now share responsibility for work evaluations with line managers.

Business, Technical, *and* Process Skills

As project management has evolved over the part 40 years, so have the skills needed by effective project managers. In the early days, the emphasis was on the technical skills of the project manager. Later, project teams began to involve more and more nontechnical people, and for the project manager behavioral skills (communication, for example) became as essential for success as technical skills. It became apparent that project managers no longer needed to be technical experts; they needed to understand technology. Besides, the projects were becoming so large and complex that one person could not possibly have all the technical knowledge needed.

What we call modern project management today puts more emphasis on business objectives than on technical ones. The current skill set includes knowledge of the business of the company, risk management expertise, and process integration skills. Project managers are now expected to be business people in addition to being technical people.

Education and Training

Project management education and training are critical in modern project management. Few training programs were available during the early years, and those that did exist emphasized the technical aspects of project management: planning, scheduling, and cost control. But today college and master's level training is available. The introduction of the project management certification program in 1985 accelerated the development of project management coursework. And more and more training in the behavioral skills needed by project managers was offered. Today's curriculums include classes on internal and external project management and emphasize behavioral over technical skills. The certification procedure has been refined, and some companies have even set up their own internal certification programs.

Project Planning Emphasized

During the early years of project management, companies spent only about 15 to 20 percent of total labor hours and dollars in planning projects. Replanning and massive scope changes were the norm, and most projects were severely overmanaged. Too much time was being spent on rethinking and reworking and too little on initial planning. In modern project management, 35 to 55 percent of total project hours is spent on planning, which varies in intensity over the life of the project. Most planning effort is expended during the initial stages of the project.

Project Objectives in Business Terms

During the traditional period of project management, the objectives of a project were defined in technical terms primarily, with little business interest incorporated. The overemphasis on technology became the source of a lot of project management problems. Because of the strong technical definition, engineers were assigned as project managers even though many of them knew little about project management. Emphasis was placed on technology regardless of cost and schedule constraints. Engineers believed in reactive rather than proactive management. Quality planning was ignored, and cost overruns and schedule slippages were the norm.

Today, project objectives are based 90 percent in business terms and only 10 percent in technical terms. Project managers are selected out of a pool of project management–trained employees. Decisions are now based on sound business practices.

Multilevel Project Sponsorship

During the period of traditional project management, only the project-driven industries used project management extensively. Because projects in the 1960s and 1970s had very definable profit goals, sponsorship came primarily from corporate executives. As more nonproject-driven companies accepted project management, however, it proved impossible for senior managers to effectively sponsor all the projects going on, and projects given lower priority were assigned to middle-level sponsors.

Modern project management, which appeared on the scene in 1993 at the end of the recession, brought with it two factors that altered former views of project sponsorship. First, some small projects fell so low in the organization that a first-line supervisor could successfully perform the role of project sponsor. For example, at National City Bank there were three levels of sponsorship on each project: working sponsors, project sponsors, and executive sponsors.

The second factor came along with concurrent engineering, which required that marketing, engineering, and production personnel all be brought on board from day one of each project. With representatives from all the disciplines working together from the start, committee sponsorship became natural. The General Motors Powertrain Group and Rohm and Haas are two examples of organizations that successfully use committee sponsorship.

Project Failures Dut to Behavioral Factors

Over the years that project management has been practiced, the causes for project failure have changed. Initially, one of the main causes of project failure was inadequate schedule and estimation planning and inadequate control procedures. Later, people began to recognize the importance of behavioral skills in successful projects, although most people still believed that most failures arose from failure to control quantitative factors such as costs.

Around 1990, postproject analyses began to indicate that most failures are indeed caused by behavioral factors in project teams. Such factors include poor morale, lack of employee commitment, lack of functional commitment, poor productivity, and poor interpersonal relationships.

This is a good place to point out that complacency can undermine even the most sophisticated project management system. The symptoms of complacency?

- Failing to learn from mistakes made in earlier projects
- Losing project management knowledge
- Canceling project management training for new employees
- Spending training dollars dedicated to project management on other topics

The National Aeronautics and Space Administration is a prime example. During the 1980s, the amount of dollars spent for project management training was declining at the same time that the employees who had helped design the project management system began retiring. There were fewer project management mentors for new employees to rely on. As a result, many of the newer workers were making the same mistakes that their predecessors had made 20 years earlier.

Changing Role of Project Managers

Today, organizations realize that the entire organization can benefit from training in project management, not just the project managers. Therefore, project managers can come from anywhere in the organization. According to Brian Vannoni of General Electric Plastics:

> We have very few dedicated project managers. Our project managers might be process engineers, they might be scientists, they might be process control technicians, maintenance mechanics, degreed or nondegreed people. A short answer for GE Plastics is that anyone, any level, any function could be called upon to lead a project.

Rose Russett, of the General Motors Powertrain Group, emphasizes not only knowledge of the business as a prerequisite for assuming the role of project manager, but also integration and behavioral skills as well:

> In the past, we had project managers that were only responsible for the deliverables within their specific function—product engineering or manufacturing engineering, for example. We now appoint a single, focal point program manager who is responsible for the entire program from beginning to end. They are the integrators of all functional deliverables and must understand all of the various functions, their interrelationships, and have the ability to work within a strong matrix organization. This integration ability is a key success factor for our program managers. The ability to work in a team environment is also critical. Our organizational structure emphasizes cross-functional teams at all levels. Our executive sponsors are by design a small, cross-functional team. The individuals that are chosen as program managers all have multifunctional backgrounds. Many have held assignments in engineering, manufacturing, quality systems, etc. This is not an entry-level position. Their skills at the behavioral side of project management such as managing and

motivating teams, communication, and conflict resolution become as important as the knowledge of the business itself when working in a project environment.

As project managers are given more and more responsibility, they are also being allowed to assume responsibility for wage and salary administration. Companies excellent in project management are still struggling with this new approach. The first problem is that the project manager may not be on the management pay scale in the company but is still being given the authority to sign off on performance evaluations. The second problem is determining which method of evaluation should be used for union employees. This problem is probably the more serious one, and the jury hasn't come in yet on what works and what doesn't. In fact, most companies haven't even addressed this problem yet.

Excellence in Modern Project Management

Companies that have achieved excellence in project management are not content to merely match their competition. Their goal is to exceed the performance of their competitors. To accomplish this goal, improvements in project management processes and systems must foster continuous success rather than sporadic success.

In Chapter 1, I introduced the idea of a hexagon of excellence: six components identified as the areas in which companies excellent in project management surpass their competitors.

- Integrated processes
- Culture
- Management support
- Education and training
- Informal project management
- Behavioral excellence

Chapters 7 through 12 will examine these components in detail.

Integrated Management Processes

As we discussed in Chapter 6, several new management processes since 1985 (concurrent engineering, for example) have supported the acceptance of project management. The most important complementary management processes, and the years they were introduced, are listed below:

- 1985: Total quality management
- 1990: Concurrent engineering
- 1991: Self-directed teams
- 1992: Employee empowerment
- 1993: Reengineering
- 1994: Life cycle costing
- 1995: Risk management
- 1995: Change management

The integration of project management with these other management processes is key to achieving excellence. Not every company uses every process all the time. Companies choose the processes that work the best for them.

The ability to integrate processes is based on which processes the company decides to implement. For example, if a company implemented a stage-gate model for project management, the company might find it an easy task to integrate new processes such as concurrent engineering. The only precondition would be that the new processes were not treated as independent functions but were designed from the onset to be part of a project management system already in place. For example, the four-phase model used by the General Motors Powertrain Group and the PROPS model used at Ericsson Telecom AB readily allow the assimilation of additional management processes.

This chapter discusses each of the management processes listed and how the processes enhance project management. Then we look at how some of the integrated management processes have succeeded in actual case studies.

Evolution of Complementary Management Processes

Since 1985, several new management processes have evolved parallel to project management. Of the eight processes we'll discuss, total quality management and concurrent engineering are the most relevant. Companies that reach excellence are the quickest to recognize the synergy among the many management options available today.

For example, consider the seven items below. Are these items part of project management or total quality management?

- Teamwork
- Strategic integration
- Continuous improvement
- Respect for people
- Customer focus
- Management by fact
- Structured problem solving

Actually, they are the primary elements of Sprint's total quality management process, but they could just as easily be listed as the facets of a project management system.

Kodak offers a course entitled Quality Leadership. The five principles behind the course are:

- Customer focus: "We will focus on our customers, both internal and external, whose inputs drive the design of products and services. The quality of our products and services is determined solely by these customers."
- Management leadership: "We will demonstrate, at all levels, visible leadership in managing by these principles."
- Teamwork: "We will work together, combining our ideas and skills to improve the quality of our work. We will reinforce and reward quality improvement contributions."

- Analytical approach: "We will use statistical methods to control and improve our processes. Data-based analyses will direct our decisions."
- Continuous improvement: "We will actively pursue quality improvement through a continuous cycle that focuses on planning, implementing, and verifying improvements in key processes."

Sound familiar?

Figure 7-1 illustrates what happens when an organization does not integrate its management processes. Separate systems may mean duplication of effort, duplication of resources, and even duplication of facilities.

Figure 7-1   Lack of integration of processes.

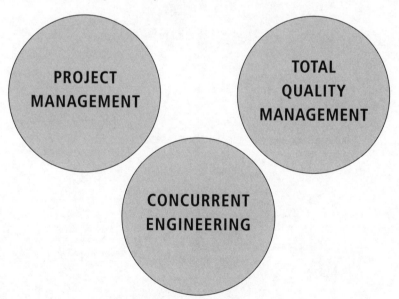

As companies recognize the synergistic effects of combining management processes into one system, usually the first two processes to be integrated are project management and total quality management. (See Figure 7-2.) As the benefits of integration become apparent, organizations choose to integrate all of the management processes. (See Figure 7-3.)

Figure 7-2   Partially integrated management processes.

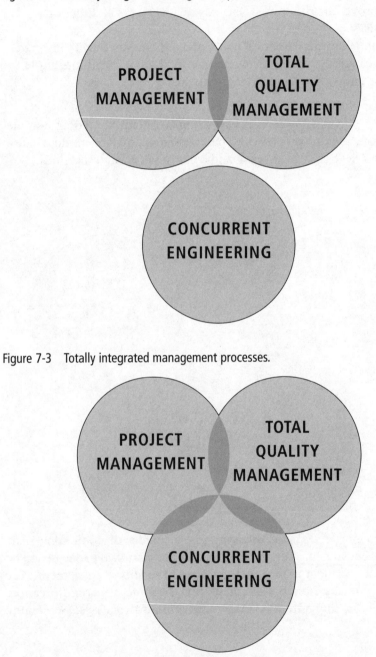

Figure 7-3   Totally integrated management processes.

Excellent companies are able to recognize the need for new processes and integrate them quickly into existing management structures. During the early 1990s, integrating project management with total quality management and concurrent engineering was emphasized. Since the middle 1990s, two other processes have become important in addition: risk management and change management. Neither of these processes is new; it's the emphasis that's new.

The importance of risk management is finally being recognized. According to Frank T. Anbari, project manager-technical systems for the National Railroad Passenger Corporation of Amtrak,

> By definition, projects are risky endeavors. They aim to create new and unique products, services, and processes that did not exist in the past. Therefore, careful management of project risk is imperative to repeatable success. Quantitative methods play an important role in risk management. There is no substitute for profound knowledge of these tools.

Risk management has been a primary focus among health care organizations for decades, and for obvious reasons. Today, in organizations of all kinds, risk management keeps us from pushing our problems downstream in the hope of finding an easy solution later on or of the problem simply going away by itself. Change management as a complement to project management is used to control the adverse effects of scope creep: increased costs (sometimes double or triple the original budget) and delayed schedules. With change management processes in place as part of the overall project management system, changes in the scope of the original project can be treated as separate projects or subprojects so that the objectives of the original project are not lost.

Today, excellent companies integrate five main management processes (see Figure 7-4):

- Project management
- Total quality management
- Concurrent engineering
- Risk management
- Change management

Figure 7-4   Integrated processes of the 1990s.

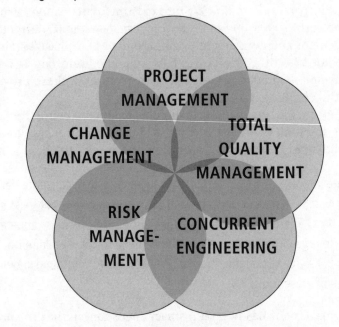

Self-managed work teams, employee empowerment, reengineering, and life-cycle costing are also combined with project management in some companies. We'll briefly discuss these less widely used processes after we have discussed the more commonly used ones.

Total Quality Management

During the past decade, the concept of total quality management has revolutionized the operations and manufacturing functions of many companies. Companies have learned quickly that project management principles and systems can be used to support and administer total quality management programs and vice versa. Ultimately, excellent companies have completely integrated the two complementary systems.

The emphasis in total quality management is on addressing quality issues in total systems. *Quality*, however, is never an end goal. Total quality management systems run continuously and concurrently in every area in which a company does business. Their goal is to bring to market products of better and better quality and not just of the same quality as last year or the year before.

Total quality management (often referred to as TQM) was founded on the principles advocated by W. Edwards Deming, Joseph M. Juran, and Phillip B. Crosby. Deming is famous for his role in turning postwar Japan into a dominant force in the world economy. Total quality management processes are based on Deming's simple plan–do–check–act cycle. (See Figure 7-5.)

Figure 7-5   The Deming plan–do–check–act cycle.

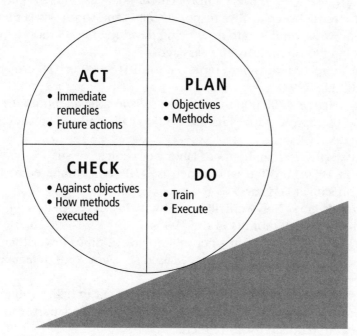

The cycle fits completely with project management principles. To fulfill the goals of any project, first you plan what you're going to do, then you do it. Next, you check on what you did. You fix what didn't work, then you execute what you set out to do. But the cycle doesn't end with the output. Deming's cycle works as a continuous improvement system, too. When the project is complete, you examine the lessons learned in its planning and execution. Then you incorporate those lessons into the process and begin the plan–do–check–act cycle all over again on a new project.

Many companies have achieved improvements using TQM. Here are only a sample (taken from C. Carl Pegels, *Total Quality Management,* Boyd and Fraser, 1994, p. 27).

- *AMP.* On-time shipments improved from 65 percent to 95 percent and AMP products have nationwide availability within three days or less on 50 percent of AMP sales.
- *Asia, Brown, Boveri.* Every improvement goal customers asked for—better delivery, quality responsiveness, and so on—was met.
- *Chrysler.* New vehicles are now being developed in 33 months versus as long as 60 months 10 years ago.
- *Eaton.* Increased sales per employee from $65,000 in 1983 to about $100,000 in 1992.
- *Fidelity.* Handles 200,000 information calls in four telephone centers; 1,200 representatives handle 75,000 calls, and the balance is automated.
- *Ford.* Use of 7.25 man-hours of labor per vehicle versus 15 man-hours in 1980; Ford Taurus bumper uses 10 parts compared to 100 parts on similar GM cars.
- *General Motors.* New vehicles are now being developed in 34 months versus 48 months in the 1980s.
- *IBM Rochester.* Defect rates per million are 32 times lower than four years ago and on some products exceed six sigma (3.4 defects per million).
- *Pratt & Whitney.* Defect rate per million was cut in half; a tooling process was shortened from two months to two days: part lead times were reduced by 43 percent.
- *VF Corp.* Market response system enables 97 percent in-stock rate for retail stores compared to 70 percent industry average.
- *NCR.* Checkout terminal was designed in 22 months versus 44 months and contained 85 percent fewer parts than its predecessor.
- *AT&T.* Redesign of telephone switch computer completed in 18 months versus 36 months, manufacturing defects reduced by 87 percent.

- *Deere & Co.* Reduced cycle time of some of its products by 60 percent, saving 30 percent of usual development costs.

Total quality management also is based on three other important elements: customer focus, process thinking, and variation reduction. Does that remind you of project management principles? It should.

One of the characteristics of companies that have won the prestigious Malcolm Baldrige Award is that each has an excellent project management system. Companies such as Motorola, Armstrong World Industries, General Motors, Kodak, Xerox, and IBM use integrated total quality management and project management systems.

Concurrent Engineering

The need to shorten product development time has always plagued U.S. companies. Under favorable economic conditions, corporations have deployed massive amounts of resources to address the problem of long development times. During economic downturns, however, not only are resources scarce, time becomes a critical constraint. Today, the principles of concurrent engineering have been almost universally adopted as the ideal solution to the problem.

Concurrent engineering requires performing the various steps and processes in managing a project in tandem rather than in sequence. This means that engineering, research and development, production, and marketing all are involved at the beginning of a project, before any work has been done. That is not always easy, and it can create risks as the project is carried through. Superior project planning is needed to avoid increasing the level of risk later in the project. The most serious risks are delays in bringing product to market and costs when rework is needed as a result of poor planning.

Improved planning is essential to project management. So it is no surprise that excellent companies integrate concurrent engineering and project management systems. Chrysler Motors used concurrent engineering with project management to go from concept to market with the Viper sports car in less than three years. Concurrent engineering may well be the strongest driving force behind the increased acceptance of modern project management.

Risk Management

Risk management is an organized means of identifying and measuring risk, and developing, selecting, and managing options for handling those risks. Throughout this book, I have emphasized that tomorrow's project managers will need superior business skills in assessing and managing risk. Project managers in the past were not equipped to quantify risks, respond to risks, develop contingency plans, or keep lessons-learned records. They were forced to go to senior managers for advice on what to do when risky situations developed. Now senior managers are empowering project managers to make risk-related decisions, and that requires a project manager with solid business skills as well as technical knowledge.

On the surface, it might seem that making risk management an integral part of project planning should be relatively easy. Just identify and address risk factors before they get out of hand. Unfortunately, the reverse is likely to be the norm, at least for the foreseeable future.

Consider the following scenario. As your organization gets better and better at project management, your customers begin giving you more and more work. You're now getting contracts for turnkey projects. Before, all you had to do was deliver the product on time and you were through. Now you are responsible for project installation and start-up as well. Sometimes even for ongoing customer service.

Because the customers no longer use their own resources on the project, they worry less about how you're handling your project management system. Or you could be working for third world clients who haven't yet developed their own systems. One hundred percent of the risk for such projects is yours, especially as projects grow more complex. (See Figure 7-6.) Welcome to the 21st century.

One subcontractor received a contract to install components in a customer's new plant. The construction of the plant would be completed by a specific date. After construction was completed, the contractor would install the equipment, perform testing, and then start-up. The subcontractor would not be allowed to bill for products or services until after a successful start-up. There was also a penalty clause for late delivery.

The contractor delivered the components to the customer on time, but the components were placed in a warehouse because construction was delayed. The contractor now had a cash flow problem and potential penalty payments because of external dependencies that sat on the critical path. In other words, the contractor's schedule was being controlled by actions of others. Had the project manager performed business risk management rather than just technical risk management, these risks could have been reduced.

Figure 7-6   Future risks.

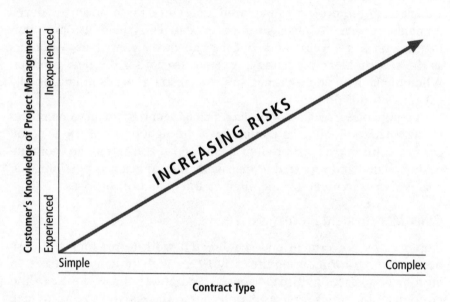

Change Management

Companies use change management to control both internally generated changes and customer-driven changes in the scope of projects. Most companies establish a configuration control board or change control board to regulate changes. For customer-driven changes, the customer participates as a member of the configuration control board.

There are at least three critical questions that must be answered by the configuration control board:

• What is the cost of the change?

- What is the impact of the change on project schedules?
- What added value does the change represent for the customer or end user?

Risk management and change management function together. Risks generate changes that, in turn, create new risks. For example, consider a company in which the project manager is given the responsibility for developing a new product. Management usually establishes a launch date even before the project is started. Management wants the income stream from the project to begin on a certain date to offset the development costs. Project managers view executives as their customers during new project development, but the executives view their customers as the stockholders expecting a revenue stream for the new product. When the launch date isn't met, surprises result in heads rolling, usually executive heads first.

In companies excellent in project management, risk management and change management occur continuously throughout the life cycle of the project. The impact on product quality, cost, and timing are continuously updated and reported to management as quickly as possible. The goal is always to minimize the number and extent of surprises.

Other Management Processes

Employee empowerment and self-directed work teams took the business world by storm during the early 1990s. With growing emphasis on customer satisfaction, it made sense to empower those closest to the customer—the order services people, nurses, clerks, and so on—to take action in solving customers' complaints. A logical extension of employee empowerment is the self-managed work team. A self-directed work team is a group of employees with given day-to-day responsibility for managing themselves and the work they perform. This includes the responsibility for handling resources and solving problems.

Some call empowerment a basis for the next industrial revolution, and it is true that many internationally known corporations have established self-directed work teams. Such corporations include Esso, Lockheed-Martin, Honeywell, and Weyerhauser. Time will tell whether these concepts turn out to be a trend or only a fad.

Reengineering a corporation is another term for downsizing the organization with the (often unfortunate) belief that the same amount of work can be performed with fewer people, at lower cost, and in a shorter period of time. Because project management proposes getting more done in less time with fewer people, it seems only practical to implement project management as part of reengineering. It still isn't certain that downsizing executed at the same time as the implementation of project management works, but project-driven organizations seem to consider it successful.

Life cycle costing was first used in military organizations. Simply stated, life cycle costing requires that decisions made during the research and development process be evaluated against the total life cycle cost of the system. Life cycle costs are the total cost to the organization for the ownership and acquisition of the product over its full life.

Integrated Processes at Work

In Chapter 4, we discussed Key Services Corporation and its development of a project management system that included risk management and change management. It took Key about two years to reach partial acceptance of their project management philosophy.

According to the manager of program management at an automotive subcontractor:

> It took [them] approximately one year [after implementation] to reach a degree of maturity in the project management process, including the structuring of procedures, calendars, pilot programs, and encompassing all programs into a regular review [plan–do–check–act] cycle. Initial programs are currently starting second-generation cycles and grandfather programs are under lessons-learned review.

Imbedded in these comments are two important points. First, the plan–do–check–act cycle mentioned is the one W. Edwards Deming introduced for continuous improvement as part of the total quality management process. Second, lessons-learned reviews are part of ISO 9000 Certification as well as the Malcolm Baldrige Award criteria. The manager's comments then reflect the integration of project management and total quality management. Let's look at Johnson Controls, perhaps the best example of a company that has achieved excellence through integrating management processes.

Johnson Controls

Headquartered in Plymouth, Michigan, Johnson Controls has become the worldwide leader in supplying seats for the automobile industry. The size of the product-driven company's projects ranges from $100,000 to $600 million. The company attributes its success in improving product quality and shortening project development time to the speed with which managers understood and integrated total quality management and project management. During a live video conference on the subject "How to Achieve Maturity in Project Management," Dave Kandt, executive director of worldwide operations at Johnson Controls, commented on the reasons behind Johnson Controls' astounding success:

> We came into project management a little differently than some companies. We have combined project management and TQC [total quality control] or total quality management. Our first design and development projects in the mid '80s led us to believe that our functional departments were working pretty well separately, but we needed to have some system to bring them together. And, of course, a lot of what project management is about is getting work to flow horizontally through the company. What we did first was to contact Dr. Norman Feigenbaum, who is the granddaddy of TQC in North America who helped us to establish some systems that linked together the whole company....

> We began with our executive office, and once we had explained the principles and philosophies of project management to these people, we moved to the managers of plants, engineering managers, cost analysts, purchasing people, and, of course, project managers. Only once the foundation was laid did we proceed with project management. We then defined their role and responsibility so that the entire company would understand their role in project management

once these people began to work. The improved understanding allowed us to move to a matrix organization and eventually to a stand-alone project management department. So how well did that work? Subsequently, since the mid-'80s, we have grown from two or three projects to roughly 50 in North America and Europe. We have grown from two or three project managers to 35. I don't believe it would have been possible to manage the growth or bring home this many projects without project management systems, procedures, and people with understanding at the highest levels of the company.

... What we've learned in these last 10 years that is the most important to us, I believe, is that you begin with the systems and understanding of what you want the various people to do in the company across all functional barriers, then bring in project management training, and last, implement project management.

Of course, the people we selected for project management were absolutely critical, and we selected the right people.... Typically, they have a technical background, a marketing background, and a business and financial background. It is very hard to find these people, but we find that they have the necessary cross-functional understanding to be able to be successful in their business.

At Johnson Controls, project management and total quality management were developed concurrently. Dave Kandt was asked during the same teleconference whether companies must have a solid total quality management culture in place before they attempt the development of a project management program. He said:

I don't think that is necessary. The reason why I say that is that companies like Johnson Controls are more of the exception rather than the rule in implementing TQM and project management together.... There is no question that having TQM in place at the same time or even first would make it a little easier, but what we've learned during the recession is that if you want to compete in Europe and you want to follow ISO 9000 guidelines, it must be implemented. And using project management as the vehicle for that implementation quite often works quite well.

About whether successful project management can function within an ISO 9000 environment, Dave Kandt said: "Not only is project management consistent with ISO 9000, a lot of the systems that ISO 9000 require[s] are crucial to project management's success."

Nortel

Nortel is an international telecommunications company based in London, with U.S. operations headquartered in Richardson, Texas. The company's business is exclusively project driven. Nortel recognized that it needed a consistent, global project management system. It emphasized the following factors during the development of its new project management system:

- Development of forms
- Training and education of employees
- Development of project management standards
- Support of project management certification for project managers

The results of the new project management system included improved financial management and risk management on projects. In addition, customer relations were improved as a result of the new system. Education and training proved to be the most important steps in introducing new techniques to support the company's cultural evolution.

Nortel is now well positioned to manage risk in the next decades. According to Bill Marshall, director of project management at Nortel:

Nortel views the project manager as the risk manager. Our financial plans for projects contain a contingency line that is identified up front along with the bid. This follows a process of risk identification and exposure. Our contracts clarify the risks borne by our company and those risks not accepted. In the case where there are risks in areas where we do not have expertise, we will pass on risks in the form of subcontracts to our partners. The risks we face in the telecom industry are with our new entrant customers who tend to overestimate the tasks they can take on. To mitigate this risk, we sell turnkey solutions and take on some of the traditional telecom operator tasks. The other risk we face is in new areas of legislation and new market entrants. The greatest rewards are for the frontier builders; for example, the cable companies' entrance into the phone business. This legislation is still unfolding, and the cable operators are oftentimes making purchases in anticipation of evolving legislation. To mitigate these risks, we will hold title to the equipment and, if necessary, will buy back the products for resale and collect sufficient amounts to ensure our labor and profit components of the sale are safeguarded.

The project manager manages the risk through tight monitoring of project deliverables (both Nortel and the customer), progress costs and payments and assessment of the operational readiness of the project. Frequent project meetings and reviews are required to identify, document, and resolve project dependencies and progress issues.

BellSouth

It's not always possible to develop a companywide policy for risk management. Risk management may need to be customized for each new project. This is particularly true of large organizations. Just identifying the need for risk management and encouraging its use is a step in the right direction, even if the process can't be immediately standardized and consistently integrated with the company's project management system.

BellSouth is a good example of such a large organization. The telecommunications company is headquartered in Atlanta, Georgia. Its project management system is used for internal customers only. Projects range in size from $1 million to $400 million.

According to Ed Prieto, director of BellSouth's corporate project management office:

> The risk management process is the responsibility of each BellSouth project manager and project team to ensure a successful project outcome. It is the project manager's responsibility to establish suitable mitigation strategies to deal with the likelihood of their occurrence. Although there is no standard procedure in place for risk management, various techniques and approaches are being reviewed by the BellSouth corporate project management office for future implementation as the standard for BellSouth. We are committed to have risk management procedures in place that will enable the project manager to identify critical risk areas, take effective risk mitigation actions, and make timely decisions regarding needed resources and priorities for risk handling. Risk management in BellSouth will be a continuous proactive process, designed to develop targeted risk reduction measures with clearly identified mitigation tasks, responsibilities, and closure dates.

Armstrong World Industries

Armstrong World Industries, a large company headquartered in Lancaster, Pennsylvania, uses project management for its own internal programs. The size of its internal projects ranges from $500,000 to $600 million. The company not only has achieved excellence in project management, it has also won the prestigious Malcolm Baldrige Award.

According to Stephen J. Senkowski, vice president for innovation processes in Armstrong's building products division:

> Our risk management tool is a financial analysis model specifically developed for new product development, as well as a financial model used for major capital investments for engineering project management. In new product development, the first step in using these financial analysis tools begins with the global marketing group identifying key major development efforts that could be undertaken and evaluating these against each other on the basis of

potential sales volume, resources required to develop and launch the product, time to develop the product, and a product probability evaluation of both the potential market success, as well as the technical and manufacturing success of the product. These are then stack ranked against one another and discussed for potential commissioning as projects in our multifunctional global new product tactical team, which includes middle management representatives from marketing, manufacturing, logistics, engineering, research, and product design.

The financial analysis is then done on a more detailed basis once the project team is formed and a kickoff and planning meeting is held with all the key constituents involved. This financial analysis is then used as a benchmark throughout the development project to determine if the project should be continued at various milestones along the way.

Before and during the project, depending on the type of product being developed, market research would be used to verify marketplace desire/acceptance so that as the product is finally developed and launched, the sales positioning can be done to maximize its return.

It should be noted that all the financial and capital investment analysis used includes extensive sensitivity analysis for items such as capital, product cost, and product sales.

To ensure a product is not going to cause a safety or environmental problem in the marketplace, a thorough product safety and design review is held with key people from quality control, product environmental, marketing, research, and legal to review all potential implications of new products. With the exception of the review of potential product categories to be developed by the global marketing team, a project manager is involved and, in most cases, coordinated the activity around these risk management tools.

Boeing Aircraft

As companies become successful in project management, risk management becomes a structured process that is performed continuously throughout the life cycle of the project. The two most common factors supporting the need for continuous risk management are how long the project lasts and how much money is at stake. For example, consider Boeing's aircraft projects. Designing and delivering a new plane might require 10 years and a financial investment of more than $5 billion.

Table 7-1 shows the characteristics of risks at Boeing. (The table does not mean to imply that risks are mutually exclusive of each other.) New technologies can appease customers, but production risks increase because the learning curve is lengthened with new technology compared to accepted technology. The learning curve can be lengthened further when features are custom-designed for individual customers. In addition, the loss of suppliers over the life of a plane can affect the level of technical and production risk. The relationships among these risks require the use of a risk management matrix and continuous risk assessment.

Table 7-1.   Risk categories at Boeing.

Type of Risk	Risk Description	Risk Mitigation Strategy
Financial	Up-front funding and payback period based upon number of planes sold	• Funding by life cycle phases • Continuous financial risk management • Sharing risks with subcontractors • Risk reevaluation based upon sales commitments
Market	Forecasting customers' expectations on cost, configuration, and amenities based on a 30-40-year life of a plane	• Close customer contact and input • Willingness to custom-design per customer • Develop a baseline design that allows for customization

Table 7-1.   (continued)

Type of Risk	Risk Description	Risk Mitigation Strategy
Technical	Because of the long lifetime for a plane, must forecast technology and its impact on cost, safety, reliability, and maintainability	• A structured change management process • Using proven technology rather than high-risk technology • Parallel product improvement and new product development processes
Production	Coordination of manufacturing and assembly of a large number of subcontractors without impacting cost, schedule, quality, or safety	• Close working relationships with subcontractors • A structured change management process • Lessons learned from other new airplane programs • Use of learning curves

Motorola

Martin O'Sullivan, vice president and director of business process management at Motorola, describes Motorola's risk management processes:

> The components of the risk management process are illustrated in [Table 7-2]. They are the risk management plan, risk identification, risk assessment, risk management planning, and overall management and reporting. The process is observed formally on large, complex projects and less formally on less complex ones.
>
> Risk identification systematically identifies the possible sources of risk and assesses the probability of occurrence and possible impact in terms of technical, schedule, and cost. Risk assessment involves the categorization of risks into risk types and areas.
>
> Project risk identification and assessment is a qualitative process, concerned with identifying significant risks, estimating their proba-

bility of occurrence, evaluating the impact in terms of time, cost, and performance. It also takes into account the causes of risk, the factors driving the magnitude of impact, and the timing of the risk. The process is regarded as the essential cornerstone of risk management.

Risk management planning involved the prioritization of risks and the allocation of resources used to control risk. Overall management and reporting defines the risk management organization, the meetings that take place, and the reports that are generated and receive management review.

Table 7-2.   Formal approach to risk management at Motorola.

Regular Updates	Risk Identification	Risk Assessment	Risk Management Planning	Overall Management and Reporting
Established strategy for project	Select and brief key staff	Evaluate individual risks, using prob-impact score	Assign risk owners	Risk register
Update as necessary	Free-format questionnaires		Prioritize risks	Risk management report
	Prompt lists	Identify major risk areas and types	Establish risk reduction actions based on urgency and manageability	Risk review board meeting
	Expert interviews	Quantify risks in terms of cost, time, and performance	Determine fallback plans	
	Check lists	Highlight critical activities		
Risk Evaluation and Management Information Systems (REMIS)				

United Technologies Automotive

Robert V. Sweeney, manager of the program management office at United Technologies Automotive (a subsidiary of United Technologies Corporation), describes the company's risk management process:

> Our overall program management approach starts with our product development & launch process (PDLP). In PDLP, there are five phases; across the five phases are eight management gateways reviews (MGRs). MGRs are strategically scheduled in the program to assess where the program is, and specifically address any risk areas that threaten the success of the program, at that point or in the future. This is attended by the program manager, the product development team (PDT) vice president, the general manager, functional representation from the Centers of Excellence (COE), and a video conference with our plant sites (Mexico, Honduras, Argentina, and the Philippines). The common document is our "MGR Package," which is a series of forms and checklists that the PDT, as a team, fills out and submits to the MGR meeting. This is made available to the PDT electronically via the program management office.
>
> Initially, risk in the program is assessed on the MGR checklist, on the order of high/medium/low, relative to timing, cost, and quality. This is accompanied by a brief narrative/description. Later in the MGR package, a risk assessment form is filled out and is specific to the functional areas of the PDT. Any risk a team member deems medium or high is recorded and described, as well as the action plan to mitigate the risk. Note that only "medium" or "high" risks are discussed since "low risk" items reside within the PDT's responsibility.
>
> Senior managers (PDT, VP, general manager, and COE directors) serve several functions in the MGR relative to assessed problems and risks. They may offer extra resources to accomplish or expedite an action plan (for example, the director of manufacturing engineering volunteering her staff to go to the plant sites to ensure their

acquisition of, and adherence to, a new assembly technique/procedure). Often they come to an MGR equipped with information that is vital but unknown to the PDT (a new technology just recently "on the shelf"). In the end, the perspectives (senior management and the PDT) are integrated, consensus established, and efforts directed or redirected.

Chapter 8

Culture

Change is a fact of life in project-driven organizations. Excellent companies know that competitive success can be achieved only when the organization has created a culture that promotes appropriate behavior from everyone in the company. Corporate cultures can't be changed overnight. They change over years.

The successful implementation of project management usually requires cultural change. Excellence in project management is achieved when the culture of the company is able to change quickly to handle the demands of new and multiple projects. Yet the culture must also be equipped to adapt to the constantly evolving and dynamic business environment. Excellent companies can cope with change in real time and live with the potential chaos that comes with it.

But change can be derailed when even one executive refuses to support the new culture. Remember that at Roadway Express, *every* executive was trained in project management. The president required it, with no exceptions. It is common practice in excellent companies that individuals who are not "on board" with the change may face disciplinary action.

This chapter discusses the importance of culture in organizations that use project management systems. The significance of corporate values, shared accountability, multiple reporting relationships, prioritization of work, and the changing role of project managers are also examined.

Creation of Corporate Culture

Corporate cultures take a long time to put into place, but they can be torn down overnight. Corporate cultures that support project management are based more on organizational behavior than on the organization's processes. And executives, managers, and staff employees must understand and accept the changes in culture needed if project management is to be successful.

Let's look at an example. In the early days of project management, a small aerospace company had to develop a project management culture if the company was to survive. The change was rapid. Unfortunately, the vice president for engineering refused to buy in to the new culture. Before the changeover to project management, the power base in the organization had been engineering. All decisions had been instigated by or approved by engineering. How did the organization get the vice president to accept the new project management culture?

The president of the company was stymied for a workable solution. Dismissing the vice president was one option, but it was impractical given the vice president's successful record and knowledge of technology. Then a solution appeared: The corporation was awarded a strategically important two-year project. The president temporarily assigned the vice president to be the project's manager and removed him from his position as vice president of engineering. By the time the project was complete, the vice president was a believer in project management and the new culture. He was promoted to the newly created position of vice president of project management.

Project management can't be copied from one company to another. Each organization is unique. But benchmarking best practices in leadership, management, and operations against competing organizations may be helpful. Companies such as United Technologies Automotive have established centers of excellence to perform continuous benchmarking.

Corporate Values

A vital element of corporate culture in excellent companies is an established set of values that all employees respect. Values are more than standard practice manuals or ethical guidelines for dealing with customers. Ensuring that the company's values and project management system are compatible contributes to the success of every project.

Successful project management can flourish within any structure, no matter how terrible the structure looks on paper. But the culture within the organization must support the four basic values of project management:

- Cooperation
- Teamwork
- Trust
- Effective communication

Here's an example of values at work. ChoiceCare of Cincinnati, Ohio, has done an outstanding job of establishing its corporate credo. When a decision needs to be made at ChoiceCare, the interest of the customers comes first. The interests of ChoiceCare come second, and the interests of the employees come third. Abiding by these values actually speeds up the decision-making process and simplifies both decision making and the planning process.

Christine Dombrowski, director of product development at ChoiceCare, explains how values work as part of ChoiceCare's project management culture:

> [Our corporate credo helps us] … because it prevents employees from thinking only of what would work best in their own department and, instead, focusing on what works best for the customer. We are very careful not to take for granted what we believe a customer might want but to instead research what their requirements are. For instance, in installing a new health plan for a customer, we would try to find out what is the preferred method of working with their staff and their employees instead of assuming they would want to use a standard process that we have. We are very careful to try to discern what the customer's requirements are and then match those inside of the organization instead of just allowing ChoiceCare just to do things the way we have always done them.

Superficially, a set of values like ChoiceCare's might imply that the customer is always right and so scope creep must be allowed to continue over the life of the project to placate the customer. This is certainly not the case. Virtually all of the companies excellent in project management practice change management to control changes in scope.

The two most common methods for managing scope changes are (1) allowing no changes after a specified point in the project's life cycle and (2) using enhancement projects. (Enhancement projects include subprojects and new projects developed parallel to the original project.)

The first method is demonstrated by Roadway Express's change management system. According to Kelly Baumer, director of project integration at Roadway:

> At Roadway Express, the design document is presented to all management groups that will be involved in the new reengineered process/system/product. Sign-off is obtained from the key users. This helps prevent scope creep. Any changes after sign-off must be separately justified after implementation.

Linda Kretz, of 20/20 Solutions in Atlanta, Georgia, described what she did to control customer-requested scope changes:

> [Scope change] has been a problem for us frequently. What we've done is insisted that our folks establish controls up front in the project to address the possibility of creeping scope. And we might define in the objectives that certain changes may be allowed up to a certain point in the project, and that beyond a certain time we cannot accept changes without going back to the client and renegotiating exactly what the outcome is going to be because it may affect the budget or the cost. But we do not arbitrarily accept the changes with the original scope of work because you are doomed to failure if you do. So, setting those controls up front really does take care of it a lot of the time.

The second method of controlling scope creep involves using enhancement projects. For example, the director of information services for an appliance manufacturer was assigned the task of preparing a uniform software package. The package had to be usable at all of the company's manufacturing plants. Representatives from the plants met and agreed to the project's scope. When the project was about three-quarters complete, scope change requests began coming in from the plants.

Managers at the plants claimed that the original scope of the project was too limited and that changes had to be made. The director of information services held her ground, asserting that she would install the software according to the original scope plan. The managers were furious. But after the software was up and running, they admitted that they could live with it. An enhancement package was discussed, which would have made some of the changes the managers wanted, but it still hasn't been submitted for approval.

Shared Accountability and Multiple Reporting Relationships

Within excellent companies, project management evolves into a behavioral culture based on multiple reporting relationships. The significance of multiple reporting relationships can't be overstated. Multiple reporting relationships must be based on a clear understanding of authority, responsibility, and accountability.

As noted in Chapter 5:

$$Accountability = Authority + Responsibility$$

The majority of the organization's resources are directly controlled by functional line managers. The line managers gain authority by virtue of their control over the resources. But the project managers still hold responsibility for the success of the projects. In excellent companies, accountability often is shared equally between the project managers and the line managers. Line managers are accountable for providing the promised resources and deliverables to the projects. Project managers are accountable to their executives and their customers for the success of their projects.

When accountability is shared, project managers no longer need to have technical expertise. Line managers are the technical experts. Today, more and more new project managers are being recruited for their business experience.

> Given shared accountability, project managers should negotiate for deliverables and the line managers' ability to get the job done within time, cost, and quality constraints. Project managers should not arbitrarily argue for the best resources available.

Shared Rewards

Shared rewards are the logical extension of shared accountability. Excellent companies never reward project managers at the expense of line managers and employees. The experience of one company is a lesson for us all.

This company, in Baltimore, had gone to project management. At its Christmas party in December 1989, the president stood up and invited three of the project managers to come to the podium. He handed each of them a check, telling each one that he had done a fantastic job on his project. Everyone in the audience applauded. The next day when the project managers arrived for work, they found that the line managers they had been working closely with had shut down work on their projects. The president of the company had a hard time understanding what he had done wrong.

Project management advocates a true team spirit, implies team management, and champions cooperation. We want line managers and project managers to see each other as peers. But that can't happen if only a few chosen members of the team are rewarded by the company. Without the line managers and the rest of the project team, the project manager could achieve nothing. In project management, you should reward the whole team or reward no one.

Team Effort and Shared Decision Making

Shared accountability fosters a close working relationship between project managers and line managers. One project manager for a defense contractor managed one of the company's four high-priority projects. The line manager she worked with shared accountability with all four of the project managers for all four of the high-priority jobs. The line manager convened a meeting to let the project managers know that she didn't have enough resources to meet the deliverable commitments she had made with the managers. Twenty people were needed for the next four months, but only 12 were available.

Senior managers might have decided to rank the projects. Then the line manager, after being notified of the priority rankings, could have decided how many people to assign to which projects. But the line manager left it up to the project managers to decide. After an hour's conversation, the four project managers told the line manager how to assign her 12 people over the next four months.

This is project management at work. Line managers go first to the project manager when a problem comes up. Project managers go first to the line manager. Problems are best solved at the lowest possible levels, and executives and project sponsors should be brought in to make decisions only if the lower-level managers can't come to a consensus. In this case, the line manager knew that the project managers had made contingency plans, and it was only a matter of putting the plans into coordinated action. (Behavioral excellence will be discussed further in Chapter 12.) Shared accountability leads to shared decision making, and shared decision making leads to excellence.

Prioritization of Work

Strong project management cultures minimize the need to prioritize work. Many projects do not need to be prioritized, but there are times when priorities are helpful. For example, a household fixture manufacturer hired an outside consultant to help improve the poor behavioral culture in the engineering division. Every engineer the consultant interviewed blamed the problems they were having on the marketing department, which kept meddling with engineering's schedules. Every interview with a marketer, however, suggested a different problem.

The company participated in two trade shows per year at which the company's new products were introduced to the market. When a new product missed its launch window at one trade show, the product could not be promoted again for six months.

On the surface, the solution might seem simple enough: Just get engineering and marketing to work together on setting launch dates. But the consultant kept digging for more information and ultimately identified the real problem. Engineering had a backup of more than 400 projects, and there were no established priorities. The engineers worked on whatever projects they wanted to.

The company's first attempt to solve the problem was to assign the top 100 projects highest priority. But once the company's project management system became established, only 20 projects could be assigned the highest priority at one time, no matter how many other projects were waiting to be finished. The point of this story? Cooperative project management cultures minimize the need to establish priorities and foster a can-do attitude among employees.

Corporate Culture at Work

Let's look at five different companies to understand how a project management culture can be firmly established companywide.

Radian International

Radian International is a medium-size, international organization with corporate headquarters in Austin, Texas. It provides consulting services on project management and technical issues to external clients. Radian is a project-driven company, and its projects range in size between $2,000 and $2 million.

Radian's corporate structure and culture are based on the concept of pool management. All of the company's human resources are organized into groups called pools. Then project managers choose the resources for their projects from a pool of resources. Internally, the company refers to this structure as resource management.

Project managers are the heart of Radian's culture. In traditional management, each manager oversees the work of five to seven employees. At Radian, the manager-to-employee ratio can be as high as 1 to 100. The project managers have the authority to negotiate with virtually any employee in any division or pool. Employees discuss their availability for a new project with project managers. When employees decide to take part in a project manager's new project, they must then commit themselves to the achievement of assigned deliverables on time and within the cost and quality standards established by the project manager. This agreement functions as an unwritten contract between employee and project manager.

Radian is very selective in the people it hires. All prospective employees are evaluated by selected members of the resource pool in which they would be employed. If the cultural fit between the pool and the candidate isn't strong enough, the candidate won't be hired.

Project managers evaluate the performance of team members at the end of each project. When an employee consistently misses deliverables, project managers stop seeking out the employee for their projects. Eventually, the employee runs out of work and may be terminated.

Project managers and employees consider each other peers. When a problem comes up on a project, literally everyone in the pool volunteers to help the project team, often on their own time. Because of the positive behavioral attitudes of Radian's employees, excellence in project management is strongly reinforced by the informal culture of the company. And teamwork, cooperation, trust, and good communication are characteristic of every resource pool.

The greatest strength of the Radian culture may well be its senior management team. Senior managers at Radian understand fully how project management should work. They empower project managers to make all decisions related to their projects. And they do not burden the project managers with excessive paperwork.

For empowerment to work, senior managers must trust project managers to make the right decisions. The empowerment of the project managers allows senior managers to act as hands-off sponsors rather than hands-on supervisors. One project manager at Radian caught the spirit of empowerment when he said, "Once a week my executive sponsor sticks his head in my office and asks if there are any problems that he should be involved with. If I say no, he leaves."

Senior managers sponsor the training programs that the employees want or need. The only restriction is that employees be willing to contribute some of their own time for training. Most of Radian's training courses are offered on Friday afternoons, evenings, and Saturdays.

The employees view Radian as a good place to work. Turnover is very low. One project manager described his experience working at Radian this way:

> Before I came to Radian, I was a middle manager with another company. I spent most of my time writing useless reports to go up and down the line in order to justify my position and that of my boss. At Radian I am a project manager and I do, in fact, manage. It is a good feeling, and it is the best job that I have ever had.

In developing its corporate culture Radian wanted to emphasize customer-focused, value-added services and flatten the organizational structure. Through providing effective training and education programs, fully adopting and trusting project management processes, and empowering project managers, the company achieved its goals. Since implementation of its project management culture, Radian has garnered happier clients, more repeat business, and fewer cost overruns and write-offs. Lessons learned? Project managers must be committed to the success of the business, and every Radian employee needs to focus on the company's clients and not on internal issues.

MidwestCorp

In general, it's safe to say that the larger the company, the more difficult it is to establish a uniform project management culture. Large companies often have pockets of effective project management, each operating separately from the others and learning their own lessons. MidwestCorp (a pseudonym) is such a company.

The large manufacturing organization operating in Ohio had one division outstanding in project management. The culture in the division was strong, and everyone in the division supported project management. The division won awards in recognition of its project management abilities. But at the same time another division of the company was about five years behind.

An audit of the poorly performing division indicated the following problems:

- Repeated process changes as new technology was adopted
- Insufficient time allocated to projects
- Too much outside interference (meetings and delays, for example)
- Schedules based on assumptions that changed as projects were executed

- Imbalance of work force
- Inconsistent objectives among work groups
- Processes that disallowed the use of freelance workers
- Inability to openly discuss issues without people feeling as though they were being personally criticized
- Lack of quality planning, scheduling, and progress tracking
- Lack of resource tracking
- Lack of supporting documentation on projects
- Need to deal with contract or agency management
- Changes or expansions of project expectations
- Constant changes in deadlines
- Last-minute changes in project requirements
- Hidden agendas
- Scopes of projects unclear from the start
- Dependence on resources without having control over them
- Fingerpointing
- No formal cost-estimating process
- Lack of understanding of work breakdowns
- Little or no customer focus
- Duplication of efforts
- No customer input
- Limited ability to support people
- Lack of management direction
- No product/project champions
- Poorly organized meetings
- Lack of cooperation
- Lack of commitment to quality
- Overlapping assignments
- Lack of management support
- Turf wars among employees
- Lack of risk management
- Scope creep
- Ineffective communications to overseas facilities
- Vague or changing responsibilities

There are situations in which a company must develop a company-wide project management culture to remain competitive. For some companies it's just keeping up with one competitor. For others, it might be keeping up with changes in the global economy. Three large companies competing with a number of competitors have done an outstanding job in developing uniform project management cultures: BellSouth, Nortel, and USAA.

BellSouth

BellSouth is a large telecommunications company headquartered in Atlanta, Georgia. It is a project management hybrid corporation, that is, it does some project-driven work, but its business is based on services and products rather than projects. All of its projects are performed for internal customers, and the projects range in size from $1 million to $400 million.

BellSouth's goal was to establish a culture to support its project management system across the organization. To accomplish that goal, the company made project management a professional discipline and instituted a continuous project management training program. BellSouth's new culture, supported by corporate sponsorship and commitment, resulted in the company's ability to meet customers' needs and even exceed their expectations.

Ed Prieto, a director in BellSouth's Strategic Management Division, offered BellSouth's story this way:

> Prior to 1994, the BellSouth project managers were responsible for the delivery of complex solutions to a diverse number of customers and project sponsors. The role of the project managers was one of project coordinator, without any authority for the project. The project manager, although skilled in the telecommunications area, lacked the knowledge to apply modern project management methodology, tools, and techniques. In fact, the project manager was not recognized in the company and did not have a career path or a clearly defined development program. Projects were completed using various methods, tools, and reporting documentation. These tools and methodologies were different from organization to organization. Confusion and inefficiency occurred due to the absence of a standard integrated methodology. Risk, quality, scope,

and scheduling control management were rarely done, with the adverse result of budget and schedule overruns on many projects. Since lessons learned and project metrics were not recorded, there is no history of project failures or successes available for measurement. The use of consultants was widespread. When an organization needed project management support, they usually hired outside consultants to manage the projects. At the end of the project, the consultants took their knowledge of project management with them.

In 1994, a corporate project initiative in the reengineering organization led the effort to implement professional project management as a discipline throughout all of BellSouth. A project management handbook was developed which combines the Project Management Institute Body of Knowledge (PMBOK), the Software Engineering Institute Capability Maturity Model (CMM), and a BellSouth management experience.

The methodology is software independent; however, MS Project is the most widely used project management software in BellSouth. The other project management software tool used is Project Workbench. A comprehensive continuing education program was established to build project management skills and knowledge. The professional development program offered by Educational Services Institute and the George Washington University leads to a Master's Certificate in Project Management.... In order to encourage employees' professional certification, an incentive cash bonus of $1,500 is awarded to project managers obtaining the Project Management Professional certification and actively managing projects. To date, over 50 BellSouth project managers hold the PMP certification, and hundreds more are preparing to sit for the exam this year.

An interest in joining PMI chapters grew as well. Recognizing the need, BellSouth established the PMI corporate-sponsored Membership Program to encourage employees' involvement in local chapter activities and to provide networking opportunities with other professionals. BellSouth also sponsored the establishment of two PMI local chapters ... and will continue to support the establishment of local chapters in BellSouth's territory.... Recognizing the value of professional project management, five levels of job descriptions for a new job family of project managers were introduced in early 1996. Realizing that to succeed in today's competitive marketplace, business must take an active part in developing the essential skills and career development needs of employees, a Project Management Career Development Program was introduced in March 1997. The program is a process which provides individuals with opportunities to develop and maintain the skills and knowledge necessary to create a level of proficiency in project management.

On January 1, 1997, the BellSouth Corporate Project Management Office was established with the mission to institutionalize modern project management discipline and techniques to effectively facilitate BellSouth's transition to an open, competitive environment. The goal of this organization is to standardize the BellSouth approach to project management by providing direction, developing and enhancing methodologies, selecting software tools, and developing guidelines to be adopted by BellSouth for use on all projects by all project management practitioners.

Project management is viewed in BellSouth as a core competency and means to increase customer satisfaction, improve efficiency in the management of projects, and improve responsiveness to customers. Our goal is to deliver consistent, professionally managed projects throughout the company, meeting cost, functionality, quality, and schedule objectives. With the support of higher management, and through the efforts of the BellSouth Corporate Project Management Office, a truly integrated project management system will be created to deliver a common approach to meet or exceed stakeholder needs and expectations from a project. Management recognizes that project management provides the skills necessary for the 21st century and is creating the mind-set to bring modern project management a reality in BellSouth.

Nortel

As an international telecommunications corporation, Nortel recognized the importance of training employees in project management skills before introducing new project management tools and techniques.

Perhaps the most difficult task confronting large corporations today is the establishment of a global culture for project management. Bill Marshall, director of project management at Nortel, explained the evolution of project management at Nortel:

> I am sure that Nortel is not alone in regards to our evolution. We tend to get pushed into our evolution in project management. It is only in the past year since we started acting globally in order to complement our global marketing story that we "have gone out of the box" and done some proactive evolution in project management. The competition of the marketplace driven by deregulation has been the push.... Nortel has broken the mold and found the formula to cooperate among the project management groups globally and to implement the standards to demonstrate global project management. In doing so, Nortel has set a new standard for project management and has gained the high ground in serving the incumbent and the new market entrant companies in the telecom business.

Chahram Bolori, vice president of Nortel Broadband Networks, describes the changing environment for Nortel and its customer contacts:

Many new market entrants are starting their telecom business spurred on by the deregulation by the World Trade Organization and countries willing to open up their markets to competition. The new entrants do not have the resources or knowledge of the incumbent telecom providers and must rely on the vendors to bring the turnkey knowledge and skills to implement complex telecom networks. Those new market entrants entering the intercountry and global telecom businesses are dependent on the vendors of standard implementation and support. Nortel project management provides a single point of contact for the customer and presents an integrated schedule and implementation plan for the total project.

David Thomas, assistant vice president for projects, at Nortel UK/ Europe, Paris, explains how this works:

The common threads of excellence in project management, work breakdown structures, financial and risk management, etc., are being applied today across the corporation to bring us all to a common baseline of terms, tools, and processes. In Europe, we have developed a project management process document that has been in use for about three years and is now being adopted globally.

We also have had a wealth of experience of managing complex projects with new telecommunications operators who are not only having to set up a network—a "relatively" straightforward project management job—but also establish their business, business processes, service offerings, organization, staffing, etc. The customer, therefore, is working in many dimensions of uncertainty at the same time. This puts him in a difficult position, because he has to manage his network supplier (Nortel) against his own framework, and that is in continuous evolution.

To the mature supplier, this is not just an opportunity to sell further services to the customer but, more importantly, it becomes a necessity to actively work with the customer to identify areas of weakness in the customer's overall plan and to find ways to provide assistance, because a failed customer will inevitably reflect on his suppliers even though the fault may not rest with them.

This requires the project managers to have additional skills and can also change the traditional relationship between customer and supplier. The project manager, being in continual contact with the customer, needs to spend time working closely with the customer, becoming part of the team, if possible, so that he can identify areas outside the contracted scope of work where Nortel can provide assistance. He then needs to describe the work proposed and sell the concept to the customer. He essentially becomes a major player in the upsell process; his role is much broader than the traditional project manager's in this type of contract. The project team also becomes much more of a partner in the overall success of the venture, rather than the traditional (often antagonistic) relationship. In fact, we have taken this as far as to have totally integrated teams (customer and Nortel), and to couple our payments to the success of the customer.

We are, therefore, having to ensure that our project managers are not only skilled in project management techniques, processes and tools, but are also skilled in sales techniques, communications, customer care and management in a supportive, constructive atmosphere.

Nortel has been very successful with the approach and has built up an excellent track record of assisting new operators with their business plans and putting them into operation through the provision of consultants or outsourcing parts of the customer operation. Perhaps the most difficult task facing large corporations today is the establishment of a global culture of project management.

Bill Marshall described how the UK/Europe experience contributed to Nortel globally and explained the underlying method:

Asia took the UK model one step further and introduced project management tools in Singapore, Malaysia, Philippines, Sri Lanka, and Thailand. The architecture was such that to achieve a roundup view, the "parent" had to contain all the data of the "children." This also required an overhead of administration to coordinate the coding structure to ensure accurate data merges. This has its drawbacks.

The future tools currently being planned will be owned by the work package owners, and a very strong public relations effort will be spent upfront to ensure buy-in. All parties up and down the information "food chain" will look at the same data but will view it in their areas of accountability. This will allow the project managers an overall view of earned value (schedule variations and cost variations). The account manager views the overall progress and exceptions. The work package owner views specific work package levels of time, cost, and quality.

Financial tools are seen as a key source of information for the project manager. The evolution of financial tools has been going on for some years, and Nortel is currently introducing a standard system into the various regions globally. This will continue until 1998.

The education tools and training must support the introduction of these new tools and culture evolution. In 1996, there were training pilots, and in 1997 all project managers will be trained in industry standards [and] 1998 will bring customized Nortel training focused on new tools and the standard Nortel processes.

The visions and plans of the project managers in Nortel are subject to funds and resource approvals. Executive support at the highest levels in Nortel is being sought to ensure this will occur in a timely and coordinated fashion. A gate process consisting of a series of decisions ensures that the key milestones for development of tools, process, and training are brought to the executives for approval. The formation of a gate process will provide up to six checkpoints for executive approvals. The frequent approvals will ensure the executives are brought into the process and are available when any of the regions step out of the model prescribed by the Global Project Management Committee.

According to Bill Marshall, "Project management is a core competency in Nortel. Centers of excellence in project management are found in the development area, internal systems support area, and the management of customer contracted services."

Bill Delroy, assistant vice president for Nortel Technology, spelled out how project management development projects:

Nortel is in the process of instilling project management as a core discipline in its reengineered product development process. Integrated product information (IPI) demands a fully committed and accountable team that takes the development project from conception through to deployment ready.

The IPI process makes it essential to have team leaders fully trained and qualified to manage a multifunctional team charged with developing for general distribution a complex high-technology product with high customer value, and this in the shortest possible time frame. The necessary skills include:

- Team formation facilitation and communication

- Risk management

- Value proposition practices

- Project estimation and planning, including resource planning

- Change management

- Financial and business management

- Uncertainty reductions

- Cost/schedule tracking and subcontract management

Training to certified levels of proficiency for team leaders is being complemented by basic training in key areas and tool usage for the team members. Complementing the training, we are defining and standardizing a common core tool set to ensure availability of accurate data and timely communications through all steps of the project.

We are working in conjunction with the more traditional users of project management represented by the market project managers to create an end-to-end capability supported by full career path, common tools, and standards that will ensure effective creation and delivery of Nortel's products and services.

The human resources side of project management is clarified by Mark Linaugh, Nortel's director of organization development:

We are training our project managers as we reengineer the process and tools for the purpose of supporting the culture shifts. The project management organizations have agreed upon standards in job profiles, pay grade levels, and skills assessments. A global standard for project management organization structures ensures the project manager has a career path. When he or she performs the current job up to expectations, the project manager knows another challenging job awaits the completion of the current project. One of the areas where project management in Nortel exceeds other companies is the area of performance against contracted expectations and control of project deliverables. The Nortel project manager measures project performance from the customer's point of view in "customer value metrics" such as performance against customer requested delivery dates.

Keith Powell, senior vice president of Nortel Information Systems and chief information officer, talked about the assess–train–mentor–certify process provided to internal project managers focused on the support tools necessary to run a global corporation:

> We assess project managers against a model, train them to a defined level of competency, mentor them to support the evolving project manager model, and certify them. This process is aligned to the project management body of knowledge of the Project Management Institute. By reaching agreement on the generic aspects of project management, Nortel enables project managers to move around the enterprise with transportable project management skills. Project management is key to Nortel delivering better, faster, more valuable solutions to its customers.

USAA

Companies that just 10 years ago saw no apparent need for project management are today reassessing their thinking. USAA is a large insurance company based in San Antonio, Texas. Its projects are performed for internal customers and range in size from thousands to millions of dollars. In 1994, USAA made the decision to adopt a project management culture to help it meet customers' expectations and keep its projects on time and within budget. To achieve its goal, the company identified project management as a formal discipline, formulated a project management training curriculum, and encouraged its employees to seek project management certification. The company found that training and education coupled with visible corporate sponsorship were the most vital elements in establishing their project management culture.

According to Colleen Andreoli, program director for the project management curriculum at USAA, this is how USAA's project management culture has evolved since 1994:

Rapidly changing and increasingly complex technology combined with the business demand for quicker solutions revitalized an interest in project management. USAA Information Systems recognized the need for project management to be a formalized discipline throughout the organization with consistent training, methodologies, and tools to ensure that projects are on schedule, within budget, and meet expectations.

In February 1994, USAA formed a working group composed of managers for IS and Information Technology Training (I/TT) staff to formulate a project management curricula. The first offering of the curricula was piloted in November 1994 for IS employees. In 1996, the program was expanded to include all business areas. To date, 104 students have graduated from the formal curriculum. The number of 1997 graduates is estimated at 96. Other significant training events in 1996 included launching an awareness level training program for project team members and functional managers, and a series of two-day executive seminars for senior management. Of note in 1997 are efforts toward utilizing in-house expertise to provide project management training instead of outsources exclusively.

To promote the benefit of networking with their peers, graduates from the curriculum established a USAA PM Forum, which meets quarterly. Guest speakers from within the organization give presentations on topics relevant to project management. There are plans to expand the program to include an electronic forum through the USAA intranet.

Also during 1994, several USAA employees participated in the founding of a PMI chapter in San Antonio....

In July of 1995, USAA approved the Project Management Professional as a recognized designation, eligible for reimbursement of expenses related to its achievement. Employees achieving the PMP are honored at the Employee Recognition Breakfast and may include the designation after their name on any company correspondence or business cards. In December 1995, 15 USAA employees sat for the exam in pursuit of their PMP certification. During 1996, 90 employees sat for the exam, including 18 executives and our CIO. To date, we have 10 PMPs and 38 others who have passed the test and are awaiting approval of their points.

Today, the job title of project manager is used only informally at USAA. However, the committee is at work exploring competencies required and an appropriate compensation plan.

This year a project was begun to "institutionalize" project management to include developing a common set of tools and processes (to be assessed through the USAA intranet), defining and supporting standardized program control, creating an in-house mentoring capability (consultants have been used to date), and creating a data repository to store current and historical project data.

Critical success factors for our evolution in project management have been the combination of both an avid grassroots movement and strong executive sponsorship. Dual sponsorship was initially provided at the vice president level. The 1996 arrival of a new CIO [a strong proponent of project management] propelled USAA's progress toward excellence. USAA regularly appears in the top 10 of *The Best U.S. Companies to Work For.* The corporate culture has a long history of supporting employee development and encouraging a learning environment.

Management
Support

As we saw in Chapter 8, senior managers are the architects of corporate culture. They are charged with making sure that their companies' cultures, once accepted, don't come apart. Visible management support is essential to maintaining a project management culture.

This chapter examines the importance of management support in the creation and maintenance of project management cultures. Case studies illustrate the vital importance of employee empowerment and the project sponsor's role in the project management system.

Visible Support from Senior Managers

As project sponsors, senior managers provide support and encouragement to the project managers and the rest of the project team. Companies excellent in project management have the following characteristics:

- Senior managers maintain a hands-off approach, but they are available when problems come up.
- Senior managers expect to be supplied with concise project status reports.
- Senior managers practice empowerment.
- Senior managers decentralize project authority and decision making.
- Senior managers expect project managers and their teams to suggest both alternatives and recommendations for solving problems, not just identification of the problems.

Robert Hershock, former vice president of 3M, said it best:

> Probably the most important thing is that they have to buy in from the top. There has to be leadership from the top, and the top has to be 100 percent supportive of this whole process. If you're a control freak, if you're someone who has high organizational skills and likes to dot all the i's and cross all the t's, this is going to be an uncomfortable process. Because basically it's a messy process, you have to have a lot of tolerance here. But what management has to do is project the confidence that they have in the teams. They have to set the strategy and the guidelines, and then they have to give the teams the empowerment that they need in order to finish their job. The best thing management can do after training the team is get out of the way.

To ensure their visibility, senior managers need to believe in walk-the-halls management. In this way, every employee will come to recognize the sponsor and realize that it is appropriate to approach the sponsor with questions. Walk-the-halls management also means that executive sponsors keep their doors open. It is important that everyone, including line managers and their employees, feels supported by the sponsor. Keeping an open door can occasionally lead to problems if employees attempt to go around lower-level managers by seeking a higher level of authority. But such instances are infrequent, and the sponsor can easily deflect the problems back to the appropriate manager.

Project Sponsorship

Executive project sponsors provide guidance for project managers and project teams. They are also responsible for making sure that the line managers who lead functional departments fulfill their commitments of resources to the projects underway. In addition, executive project sponsors maintain communication with customers. (See Figure 9-1.)

Figure 9-1 The roles of the project sponsor.

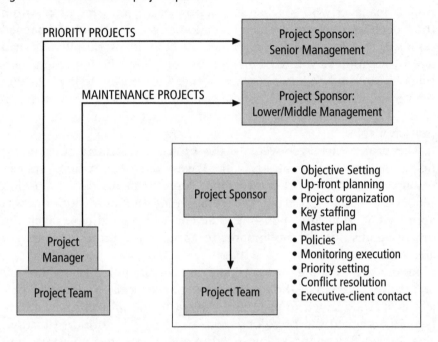

The project sponsor usually is an upper-level manager who, in addition to his or her regular responsibilities, provides ongoing guidance to assigned projects. An executive might take on sponsorship for several concurrent projects. Sometimes, on lower-priority or maintenance projects, a middle-level manager may take on the project sponsor role. One organization I know of even prefers to assign middle managers instead of executives. The company believes that avoids the common problem of lack of line manager buy-in to projects.

In some large, diversified corporations, senior managers don't have adequate time to invest in project sponsorship. In such cases, project sponsorship falls to the level below corporate senior management or to a committee.

Some projects don't need project sponsors. Generally, sponsorship is required on large, complex projects involving a heavy commitment of resources. Large, complex projects also require a sponsor to integrate the activities of the functional lines, to dispel disruptive conflicts, and to maintain strong customer relations.

Consider one example of a project sponsor's support for a project. A project manager who was handling a project in an organization within the federal government decided that another position would be needed on his team if the project was to meet its completion deadline. He had already identified a young woman in the company who fit the qualifications he had outlined. But adding another full-time-equivalent position seemed impossible. The size of the government project office was constrained by a unit-manning document that dictated the number of positions available.

The project manager went to the project's executive sponsor for help. The executive sponsor worked with the organization's human resources and personnel management department to add the position requested. Within 30 days, the addition of the new position was approved. Without the sponsor's intervention, it would have taken the organization's bureaucracy months to approve the project, too late to affect the deadline.

In another example, the president of a medium-size manufacturing company wanted to fill the role of sponsor on a special project. The project manager decided to use the president to the project's best advantage. He assigned the president/sponsor to handle a critical situation. The president/sponsor flew to the company's headquarters and returned two days later with an authorization for the new tooling the project manager needed. The company ended up saving time on the project, and the project was completed four months earlier than originally scheduled.

Sponsorship by Committee

As companies grow, it sometimes becomes impossible to assign a senior manager to every project, and so committees act in the place of individual project sponsors. In fact, the recent trend has been toward committee sponsorship in many kinds of organizations. A project sponsorship committee usually is made up of a representative from every function of the company: engineering, marketing, and production. Committees may be temporary, when a committee is brought together to sponsor one time-limited project, or permanent, when a standing committee takes on the ongoing project sponsorship of new projects.

For example, the General Motors Powertrain Group has achieved excellence in using committee sponsorship. The directors of product engineering, manufacturing engineering, and manufacturing make up the committee for new and/or major engine and transmission product programs. The program sponsors demonstrate visible executive-level project support and commitment to the entire organization. The committee's roles and responsibilities include:

- Appointing the program (or project) manager and team as part of the charter process
- Reviewing the master program plan to ensure its sufficiency
- Monitoring the execution of the program and participating in gate reviews
- Providing executive-level customer contact as needed
- Promoting and sharing lessons learned across programs

In addition to their roles as project sponsors, these directors also serve on the program management steering committee, which has the following responsibilities:

- Approving changes to the project management process
- Conducting project reviews to ensure compliance with the common project management process

Phases of Project Sponsorship

The role of the project sponsor changes over the life cycle of a project. During the planning and initiation phases, the sponsor plays an active role in the following activities:

- Helping the project manager establish the objectives of the project
- Providing guidance to the project manager during the organization and staffing phases
- Explaining to the project manager what environmental or political factors might influence the project's execution
- Establishing the project's priority (working alone or with other company executives) and then informing the project manager about the project's priority in the company and the reason that priority was assigned
- Providing guidance to the project manager in establishing the policies and procedures for the project
- Functioning as the contact point for customers and clients

During the execution phase of a project, the sponsor must be very careful in deciding which problems require his or her guidance. Trying to get involved with every problem that comes up on a project will result in micromanagement. It will also undermine the project manager's authority and make it difficult for the executive to perform his or her regular responsibilities.

For short-term projects of two years or less, it's usually best that the project sponsor assignment isn't changed over the duration of the project. For long-term projects of five years, more or less, different sponsors could be assigned for every phase of the project, if necessary. Choosing sponsors from among executives at the same corporate level works best, since sponsorship at the same level creates a "level" playing field whereas at different levels, favoritism can occur.

Project sponsors needn't come from the functional area where the majority of the project work will be completed. Some companies even go so far as assigning sponsors from line functions that have no vested interest in the project. Theoretically, this system promotes impartial decision making.

Customer Relations

The role of executive project sponsors in customer relations depends on the type of organization (entirely project driven or partially project driven) and the type of customer (external or internal). Contractors working on large projects for external customers usually depend on executive project sponsors to keep the clients fully informed of progress on their projects. Customers with multimillion-dollar projects often keep an active eye on how their money is being spent. They are relieved to have an executive sponsor they can turn to for answers.

It is common practice for contractors heavily involved in competitive bidding for contracts to include both the project manager's and the executive project sponsor's résumés in proposals. All things being equal, the résumés may give one contractor a competitive advantage over another.

Customers prefer to have a direct path of communication open to their contractors' executive managers. One contractor identified the functions of the executive project sponsor as:

- Actively participating in the preliminary sales effort and contract negotiations
- Establishing and maintaining high-level client relationships
- Assisting project managers in getting the project underway (planning, staffing, and so forth)
- Maintaining current knowledge of major project activities
- Handling major contractual matters
- Interpreting company policies for project managers
- Helping project managers identify and solve significant problems
- Keeping general managers and client managers advised of significant problems with projects

Decision Making

Imagine that project management is like car racing. A yellow flag is a warning to watch out for a problem. Yellow flags require action by the project manager or the line manager. There's nothing wrong with informing an executive about a yellow-flag problem as long as the project manager is not looking for the sponsor to solve the problem. Red flags, however, usually do require the sponsor's direct involvement. Red flags indicate problems that may affect the time, cost, and performance parameters of the project. So red flags need to be taken seriously and decisions need to be made collaboratively by the project manager and the project sponsor.

Serious problems sometimes result in serious conflicts. Disagreements between project managers and line managers are not unusual, and they require the thoughtful intervention of the executive project sponsor. First, the sponsor should make sure that the disagreement can't be solved without his or her help. Second, the sponsor needs to gather information from all sides and consider the alternatives being considered. Then, the sponsor must decide whether he or she is qualified to settle the dispute. Often, disputes are of a technical nature and require someone with the appropriate knowledge base to solve them. If the sponsor is unable to solve the problem, he or she will need to identify another source of authority who has the needed technical knowledge. Ultimately, a fair and appropriate solution can be shared by everyone involved. If there were no executive sponsor on the project, the disputing parties would be forced to go up the line of authority until they found a common superior to help them. Having executive project sponsors minimizes the number of people and the amount of time required to settle work disputes.

Strategic Planning

Executives are responsible for performing the company's strategic planning, and project managers are responsible for the operational planning on their assigned projects. Although the thought processes and time frames are different for the two types of planning, the strategic planning skills of executive sponsors can be useful to project managers. For projects that involve process or product development, sponsors can offer a special kind of market surveillance to identify new opportunities that might influence the long-term profitability of the organization. And sponsors can gain a lot of strategically important knowledge from lower-level managers and employees. Who else knows better when the organization lacks the skill and knowledge base it needs to take on a new type of product? when the company needs to hire more technically skilled labor? what technical changes are likely to affect their industry?

Excellence in Project Sponsorship

Many companies have achieved excellence in their application of project sponsorship. Radian International depends on single-project sponsors to empower their project managers for decision making. General Motors proved that sponsorship by committee works. Roadway and ChoiceCare demonstrated the vital importance of sponsorship training for both sponsorship by a single executive and sponsorship by a committee.

In excellent companies, the role of the sponsor is not to supervise the project manager but to make sure that the best interests of both the customer and the company are recognized. However, as the next two examples reveal, it's seldom possible to make executive decisions that appease everyone.

Franklin Engineering (a pseudonym) had a reputation for developing high-quality, innovative products. Unfortunately, the company paid a high price for its reputation: a large research and development budget. Fewer than 15 percent of the projects initiated by research and development led to the full commercialization of a product and the recovery of the research costs.

The company's senior managers decided to implement a policy that mandated that all research and development project sponsors periodically perform cost-benefit analyses on their projects. When a project's cost-benefit ratio failed to reach the levels prescribed in the policy, the project was canceled for the benefit of the whole company.

Initially, research and development personnel were unhappy to see their projects canceled, but they soon realized that early cancellation was better than investing large amounts in projects that were likely to fail. Eventually, the project managers and team members came to agree that it made no sense to waste resources that could be better used on more successful projects. Within two years, the organization found itself working on more projects with a higher success rate but no addition to the research and development budget.

Another disguised case involves a California-based firm that designs and manufactures computer equipment. Let's call the company Design Solutions. The research and development group and the design group were loaded with talented individuals who believed that they could do the impossible and often did. These two powerful groups had little respect for the project managers and resented schedules because they thought schedules limited their creativity.

In June 1997, the company introduced two new products that made it onto the market barely ahead of the competition. The company had planned initially to introduce them by the end of 1996. The reason for the late releases: projects had been delayed because of the project teams' desire to exceed the specifications required and not just meet them.

To help the company avoid similar delays in the future, the company decided to assign executive sponsors to every research and development project to make sure that the project teams adhered to standard management practices in the future. Some members of the teams tried to hide their successes with the rationale that they could do better. But the sponsor threatened to dismiss the employees and they eventually relented.

The lessons in both cases are clear. Executive sponsorship actually can improve existing project management systems to better serve the interests of the company and its customers.

Empowerment of Project Managers

One of the biggest problems with assigning executive sponsors to work beside line managers and project managers is the possibility that the lower-ranking managers will feel threatened with a loss of authority. This problem is real and must be dealt with at the executive level. Frank Jackson, a senior manager at MCI, believes in the idea that information is power:

> We did an audit of teams to see if we were really making the progress that we thought or were we kidding ourselves, and we got a surprising result. When we looked at the audit, we found out that 50 percent of middle management's time was spent in filtering information up and down the organization. When we had a sponsor, the information went from the team to the sponsor to the operating committee, and this created a real crisis in our middle management area.

> MCI found a solution to this problem. If there is anyone who believes that just going and dropping into a team approach environment is an easy way to move, it's definitely not. Even within the companies that I'm involved with, it's very difficult for managers to give up the authoritative responsibilities that they have had. You just have to move into it, and we've got a system where we communicate within MCI, which is MCI Mail. It's an electronic mail system. What it has enabled us to do as a company is bypass levels of management. Sometimes you get bogged down in communications, but it allows you to communicate throughout the ranks without anyone holding back information.

Not only do executives have the ability to drive project management to success, they also have the ability to create an environment that leads to project failure. According to Robert Hershock, former vice president of 3M:

Most of the experience that I had where projects failed was because of management meddling. Either management wasn't 100 percent committed to the process or management just bogged the whole process down with reports and a lot of innuendoes. The biggest failures I've seen anytime have been really because of management.... Basically, there are two experiences where projects have failed to be successful. One is the management meddling where management cannot give up its decision-making capabilities, constantly going back to the team and saying you're doing this wrong or you're doing that wrong. The other side of it is when the team can't communicate its own objective. When it can't be focused, the scope continuously expands, and you get into project creep. The team just falls apart because it has lost its focus.

Project failure can often be a matter of false perceptions. Most executives believe that they have risen to the top of their organizations as solo performers. It's very difficult for them to change without feeling that they are giving up a tremendous amount of power, which traditionally is vested in the highest level of the company. To change this situation, it may be best to start small. Frank Jackson observed:

There are so many occasions where senior executives won't go to training and won't listen, but I think the proof is in the pudding. If you want to instill project management teams in your organizations, start small. If the company won't allow you to do it using the Nike theory of just jumping in and doing it, start small and prove to them one step at a time that they can gain success. Hold the team accountable for results—it proves itself.

It's also important for us to remember that executives can have valid reasons for micromanaging. One executive commented on why project management might not be working as planned in his company:

We, the executives, wanted to empower the project managers and they, in turn, would empower their team members to make decisions as they relate to their project or function. Unfortunately, I do not feel that we [the executives] totally support decentralization of decision making due to political concerns that stem from the lack of confidence we have in our project managers who are not proactive and have not demonstrated leadership capabilities.

In most organizations, senior managers start at a point where they trust only their fellow managers. As the project management system improves and a project management culture develops, senior managers come to trust project managers even though they do not occupy positions high on the organizational chart. Empowerment doesn't happen overnight. It takes time, and unfortunately, a lot of companies never make it to full project manager empowerment. (See Figure 9-2.)

Figure 9-2 Time-dependent changes in trust.

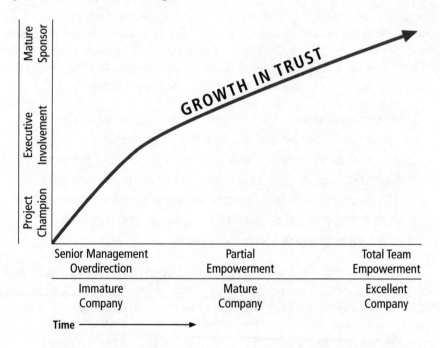

Figure 9-2 shows how this can happen over time. The top figure illustrates how, as trust develops, sponsorship moves down in the organization, rather than remaining at executive levels. In the bottom figure, we see growing trust leading toward mature sponsorship. Without trust, senior management micromanages the project and acts as a champion. As executives begin to trust the team more and more, the team achieves partial empowerment, thus proving to executives the team's ability to make decisions. With total team empowerment, executives act as mature sponsors, keeping hands off except when needed.

Management Support at Work

Visible executive support is necessary for successful project management and the stability of a project management culture. But there is such a thing as too much visibility for senior managers. Take the following case example, for instance.

Midline Bank

Midline Bank (a pseudonym) is a medium-size bank doing business in a large city in the Northwest. Executives at Midline realized that growth in the banking industry in the near future would be based on mergers and acquisitions and that Midline would need to take an aggressive stance to remain competitive. Financially, Midline was well prepared to acquire other small- and middle-size banks to grow its organization.

The bank's information technology group was given the responsibility of developing an extensive and sophisticated software package to be used in evaluating the financial health of the banks targeted for acquisition. The software package required input from virtually every functional division of Midline. Coordination of the project was expected to be difficult.

Midline's culture was dominated by large, functional empires surrounded by impenetrable walls. The software project was the first in the bank's history to require cooperation and integration among the functional groups. A full-time project manager was assigned to direct the project.

Unfortunately, Midline's executives, managers, and employees knew very little about the principles of project management. But the executives did recognize the need for executive sponsorship. A steering committee of five executives was assigned to provide support and guidance for the project manager. None of the executives understood project management. As a result, the steering committee interpreted its role as one of continuous daily direction of the project.

Each of the five executive sponsors asked for weekly personal briefings from the project manager, and each sponsor gave conflicting directions. Each executive had his or her own agenda for the project.

By the end of the project's second month, chaos took over. The project manager spent most of his time preparing status reports instead of managing the project. The executives changed the project's requirements frequently, and the organization had no change control process other than the steering committee's approval.

At the end of the fourth month, the project manager resigned and sought employment outside the company. One of the executives from the steering committee then took over the project manager's role, but only on a part-time basis. Ultimately, the project was taken over by two more project managers before it was complete, one year later than planned. The company learned a vital lesson: More sponsorship is not necessarily better than less.

Contractco

Another disguised case involves a Kentucky-based company I'll call Contractco. Contractco is in the business of nuclear fusion testing. The company was in the process of bidding on a contract with the U.S. Department of Energy. The department required that the project manager be identified as part of the company's proposal and that a list of the project manager's duties and responsibilities be included. To impress the Department of Energy, the company assigned both the executive vice president and the vice president of engineering as cosponsors.

The Department of Energy questioned the idea of dual sponsorship. It was apparent to the department that the company did not understand the concept of project sponsorship, because the roles and responsibilities of the two sponsors appeared to overlap. The department also questioned the necessity of having the executive vice president serve as a sponsor.

The contract was eventually awarded to another company. Contractco learned that a company should never underestimate the customer's knowledge of project management or project sponsorship.

Health Care Associates

Health Care Associates (a pseudonym) provides health care management services to both large and small companies in New England. The company partners with a chain of 23 hospitals in New England. More than 600 physicians are part of the professional team, and many of the physicians also serve as line managers at the company's branch offices. The physician-managers maintained their own private clinical practices as well.

It was the company's practice to use boilerplate proposals prepared by the marketing department to solicit new business. If a client was seriously interested in Health Care Associates' services, a customized proposal based on the client's needs would be prepared. Typically, the custom-design process took as long as six months or even a full year.

Health Care Associates wanted to speed up the custom-design proposal process and decided to adopt project management processes to accomplish that goal. In January 1994, the company decided that it could get a step ahead of its competition if it assigned a physician-manager as the project sponsor for every new proposal. The rationale was that the clients would be favorably impressed.

The pilot project for this approach was Sinco Energy (another pseudonym), a Boston-based company with 8,600 employees working in 12 cities in New England. Health Care Associates promised Sinco that the health care package would be ready for implementation no later than June 1994.

The project was completed almost 60 days late and substantially over budget. Health Care Associates' senior managers privately interviewed each of the employees on the Sinco project to identify the cause of the project's failure. The employees had the following observations:

- Although the physicians had been given management training, they had a great deal of difficulty applying the principles of project management. As a result, the physicians ended up playing the role of invisible sponsor instead of actively participating in the project.

- Because they were practicing physicians, the physician sponsors were not fully committed to their role as project sponsors.
- Without strong sponsorship, there is no effective process in place to control scope creep.
- The physicians had no authority over the line managers, who supplied the resources needed to complete a project successfully.

Health Care Associates' senior managers learned two lessons. First, not every manager is qualified to act as a project sponsor. Second, the project sponsors should be assigned on the basis of their ability to drive the project to success. Impressing the customer is not everything.

Training and Education

Chapter 10

Establishing project management training programs is one of the greatest challenges facing training directors, because project management involves numerous complex and interrelated skills (qualitative/behavioral, organizational, and quantitative). In the early days of project management, project managers learned by their own mistakes rather than from the experience of others. Today, companies excellent in project management are offering a corporate curriculum in project management. Effective training supports project management as a *profession*.

Some large corporations offer more internal courses related to project management than most colleges and universities do. These companies include General Electric, General Motors, Kodak, the National Cryptological School, Ford Motor Company, and USAA. Such companies treat education almost as a religion. Smaller companies have more modest internal training programs and usually send their people to publicly offered training programs.

This chapter discusses processes for identifying the need for training, selecting the students who need training, designing and conducting the training, and measuring training's return on dollars invested.

Training for Modern Project Management

During the early days of project management, in the late 1950s and 1960s, training courses concentrated on the advantages and disadvantages of various organizational forms (for example, matrix, traditional, functional). Executives learned quickly, however, that any organizational structure can be made to work effectively and efficiently when basic project management is applied. Project management skills based in trust, teamwork, cooperation, and communication can solve the worst structural problems.

Starting with the 1970s, emphasis turned away from organizational structures for project management. The old training programs were replaced with two basic programs:

- Basic project management, which stresses behavioral topics such as multiple reporting relationships, time management, leadership, conflict resolution, negotiation, team building, motivation, and basic management areas such as planning and controlling
- Advanced project management, which stresses scheduling techniques and software packages used for planning and controlling projects

Today's project management training programs include courses on behavioral as well as quantitative subjects. The most important problem facing training managers is how to achieve a workable balance between the two parts of the coursework (behavioral and quantitative). (See Figure 10-1.) For publicly sponsored training programs, the seminar leaders determine their own comfort levels in the "discretionary zone" between technical and behavioral subject matter. For in-house trainers, however, the balance must be pre-established by the training director on the basis of factors such as which students will be assigned to manage projects, types of projects, and average lengths of projects. (See Table 10-1.)

Figure 10-1 Types of project management training.

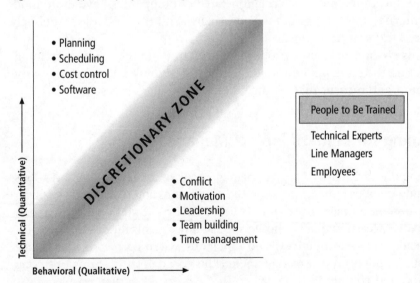

Table 10-1. Emphases in various training programs

| | Type of Person Assigned for PM Training (PM Source) | Training Program Emphasis | |
		Quantitative/ Technology Skills	Behavior Skills
NEED FOR TRAINING — To Function as a Project Manager	• Technical expert on short-term projects	High	Low
	• Technical expert on long-term projects	High	High
	• Line manager acting as a part-time project manager	High	Low
	• Line manager acting as a full-time project manager	High	Average to high
	• Employees experienced in cooperative operations	High	Average to high
	• Employees inexperienced in cooperative operations	High	Average to high
General Knowledge	• Any employees or managers	Average	Average

Identifying the Need for Training

Identifying the need for training requires that line managers and senior managers recognize two critical factors: first, that training is one of the fastest ways to build project management knowledge in a company, and, second, that training should be conducted for the benefit of the corporate bottom line through enhanced efficiency and effectiveness.

According to John Benson, a senior program manager at OEC Medical Systems:

> It took about two years [after implementation] to start bringing projects in on time. It has taken one to two more years to establish change control processes. Our company has not yet committed all functional areas of the company to project management. We are struggling to improve in that area and to formally embrace TQM and continuous improvement by training people in the company.

Selecting the Students

Selecting the people to be trained is critical. As we've already seen in a number of case studies, it's usually a mistake to train only the project managers. A thorough understanding of project management and project management skills is needed throughout the organization if project management is to be successful. For example, one automobile subcontractor invested months in training its project managers. Six months later, projects were still coming in late and over budget. The executive vice president finally realized that project management was a team effort rather than an individual responsibility. After that revelation, training was provided for all of the employees who had anything to do with the projects. Virtually overnight, project results improved.

Dave Kandt, executive director of worldwide operations at Johnson Controls, explained how his company's training plan was laid out to achieve excellence in project management:

> We began with our executive office, and once we had explained the principles and philosophies of project management to these people, we moved to the management of plants, engineering managers, cost analysts, purchasing people, and, of course, project managers. Only once the foundation was laid we proceeded with actual project management and to define the role and responsibility so that the entire company would understand their role in project management once these people began to work. Just the understanding allowed us to move to a matrix organization and eventually to a stand-alone project management department.

Designing the Courses and Conducting the Training

Many companies have come to realize that on-the-job training may be less effective than more formal training. On-the-job training virtually forces people to make mistakes as a learning experience, but what are they learning? How to make mistakes. It seems much more efficient to train people to do their jobs the right way from the start. Table 10-2 shows an abbreviated list of the courses offered by USAA, Ford Motors, and Armstrong World Industries.

Table 10-2   Typical in-house project management training programs.

USAA	
Building Effective Teams	Planning, Scheduling, and Cost
Risk Management	ITAP and Investment Workshop
The Complete Project Manager	Winning Support from Others
Communicating One-to-One	Building Collaborative Relationships
Facilitation for Leaders	Effective Writing
Coaching for Performance	Building a Foundation of Trust
Giving a Briefing	Leadership Training
Helping Your Team Reach Consensus	Resolving Team Conflicts
Making the Most of Team Differences	Negotiation
Outcome Thinking	Applying Project Workbench
Advanced Project Workbench	Microsoft Project
PMBOK Review	Business Process Reengineering
Communicating Change	Seven Steps to Change
Strategic Project Management	Multiproject Management
Managing Software Projects	Managing Client/Server Projects
Business Orientation Assignment	Interpersonal Skills

Ford	
Benchmarking	Financial Engineering
Microsoft Project	Theory of Constraints
Writing on Target	Failure Mode and Effects Analysis
ISO 9000	Quality Operating Systems

Table 10-2   (continued)

Ford (continued)	
Quick Quality Function Deployment	Reliability
Statistic Process Control	Zero Defects
Communication Skills	Achieving Win–Win Outcomes
Effective Listening and Feedback	Outstanding Meetings
Shifting the Conflict Paradigm	Successful Work Teams
Basic Supervisory Knowledge	Coaching and Counseling
Models for Management	Team-Oriented Problem Solving
Collaborative Decision Making	Working in a Matrix Organization
Working in a Multicultural Organization	Facilitation Skills
On-the-Job Training	Time Management
Waste Minimization	

Armstrong World Industries	
Project Management	Microsoft Project
Project Manager Capability Assessment	Value Analysis
Team Leadership	Time Management
Team Problem Solving for Leaders	Team Interaction Skills
Stress Management	Recognition
Presentation Skills	Performance Appraisals
Negotiation Skills	Meeting Skills
Creative Problem Solving	Facilitation
Group Dynamics	Statistical Process Control
Design of Experiments	Technical Leadership
Business Strategies/Decision Making	

Project management has become a career path. More and more companies today allow or even require that their employees get project management certification. One company informed its employees that project management certification would be treated the same as a master's degree in the salary and career-path structure. The cost of the training behind the certification process is only 5 or 10 percent of the cost of a typical master's degree in business administration program. And certification promises a quicker return on investment for the company. Project management certification can also be useful for employees without college degrees; it gives them the opportunity for a second career path within the company.

Linda Kretz, of 20/20 Solutions in Atlanta, Georgia, explained what type of project management training worked the best in her experience:

> In our experience, we have found that training them ahead of time is definitely the better route to go. We have done it the other way with people learning on the job, and that has been a rather terrifying situation at times. When we talk about training, we are not just talking about training. We want our project managers to be certified through the Project Management Institute. We have given our people two years to certify. To that end there is quite a bit of personal study required. I do believe that training from the formal training end is great and then you can modify that to whatever the need is in-house.

Rose Russett, of the General Motors Powertrain Group, described what she believes is working well for her group:

> We have a single, dedicated program manager on each of our product programs. This provides a focal point of responsibility. These individuals are chosen for their leadership skills and ability to work within our cross-functional team structure. These program managers report to an executive sponsor committee of three directors that is committed to and fully supportive of program management. When the program manager and team are appointed, they are

given training to understand the program organizational structure, roles, and responsibilities of the team, and common systems and processes that will be used throughout the life of the program. This starts the entire team out with full knowledge of how work will get done and should minimize potential ambiguity and confusion that could result when working in a matrix organizational structure.

As companies master the quantitative side of project management, the emphasis in training shifts to behavioral skills. According to Brian Vannoni of General Electric Plastics:

The behavior that we've been driving in our organizations is bound-arylessness. We are looking at driving the behaviors across the organizations such that people are comfortable interacting, matrixing, and teaming with people from any business function or discipline. Just as the degrees of project success have grown, also has the need for people to have the ability to interact with other business functions in very diverse team situations. Diversity may include other cultures due to the global nature of our business.

Over the years, we have been pursuing boundarylessness behavior and during that time we have developed and delivered approximately 50 different modules, classes, and seminars, all focused around behaviors. Some of the courses and concepts are based on Zenger Miller, Hershey/Blanchard (situational leadership), and other behavior-oriented models and material. Team skills training, facilitation training, process mapping, and interpersonal skills are key to this behavior.

Bill Marshall, director of project management for Nortel, discussed the complexities of getting a uniform methodology in place for project management when a company wishes to become a global competitor:

As our process evolves and the methods require a new culture, we are using training courses to bring about an understanding of this new culture. The International Institute of Learning is providing the basic project management training and the introduction into the new culture. These courses are being presented to the multiple global business segments headquartered in Richardson, Texas. Regions of the UK, Europe, Australia, and Central and Latin America are registered for courses in 1997. The project managers are also receiving internal training on financial management projects and a new contract ledger, instructions on contractual language, and personal development training to prepare them for holding effective meetings and dealing with difficult customers. The training of the future will be more closely aligned with the project management tools and, in fact, may be more CBT [computer-based training] with online simulations of real projects. The process-driven navigation tools associated with the customized desktop for a project manager may contain training models that can be exercised in the project manager's spare time.

There is also the question of which are better: internally based or publicly held training programs. The answer depends on the nature of the individual company and how many employees need to be trained, how big the training budget is, and how deep the company's internal knowledge base is. If only a few employees at a time need training, it might be effective to send them to a publicly sponsored training course. But if large numbers of employees need training on an ongoing basis, designing and conducting a customized internal training program might be the way to go.

In general, custom-designed courses are the most effective. In excellent companies, course content surveys are conducted at all levels of management. For example, the research and development group of Babcock and Wilcox in Alliance, Ohio, needed a project management training program for 200 engineers. The head of the training department knew that she was not qualified to select core content, and so she sent questionnaires out to executive managers, line managers, and professionals in the organization. The information from the questionnaires was used to develop three separate courses for the audience. At Ford Motor Company, training was broken down into a two-hour session for executives, a three-day program for project personnel, and a half-day session for overhead personnel.

For internal training courses, choosing the right trainers and speakers is crucial. A company can use trainers currently on staff if they have a solid knowledge of project management, or the trainers can be trained by outside consultants who offer train-the-trainer programs. Either way, trainers from within the company must have the expertise the company needs. Some problems with using internal trainers include the following:

- Internal trainers may not be experienced in all the areas of project management.
- Internal trainers may not have up-to-date knowledge of the project management techniques practiced by other companies.
- Internal trainers may have other responsibilities in the company and so may not have adequate time for preparation.
- Internal trainers may not be as dedicated to project management or as skillful as external trainers.

But the knowledge base of internal trainers can be augmented by outside trainers as necessary. In fact, most companies use external speakers and trainers for their internal educational offerings. The best way to select speakers is to seek out recommendations from training directors in other companies and teachers of university-level courses in project management. Another method is contacting speaker's bureaus, but the quality of the speaker's program may not be as high as needed. The most common method for finding speakers is reviewing the brochures of publicly sponsored seminars. Of course, the brochures were created as sales materials, and so the best way to evaluate the seminars is to attend them.

After a potential speaker has been selected, the next step is to check his or her recommendations. Table 10-3 outlines many of the pitfalls involved in choosing speakers for internal training programs and how you can avoid them.

Table 10-3. Common pitfalls in hiring external trainers and speakers.

Warning Sign	Preventive Step
Speaker professes to be an expert in several different areas.	Verify speaker's credentials. Very few people are experts in several areas. Talk to other companies that have used the speaker.
Speaker's résumé identifies several well-known and highly regarded client organizations.	See whether the speaker has done consulting for any of these companies more than once. Sometimes a speaker does a good job selling himself or herself the first time, but the company refuses to rehire him or her after viewing the first presentation.
Speaker makes a very dramatic first impression and sells himself or herself well. Brief classroom observation confirms your impression.	Being a dynamic speaker does not guarantee that quality information will be presented. Some speakers are so dynamic that the trainees do not realize until too late that "the guy was nice but the information was marginal."
Speaker's résumé shows 10 to 20 years or more experience as a project manager.	Ten to 20 years of experience in a specific industry or company does not mean that the speaker's knowledge is transferable to your company's specific needs or industry. Ask the speaker what types of projects he or she has managed.
Marketing personnel from the speaker's company aggressively show the quality of their company, rather than the quality of the speaker. The client list presented is the company's client list.	You are hiring the speaker, not the marketing representative. Ask to speak or meet with the speaker personally and look at the speaker's client list rather than the parent company's client list.
Speaker promises to custom-design his or her materials for your company's needs.	Demand to see the speaker's custom-designed material at least two weeks before the training program. Also verify the quality and professionalism of view graphs and other materials.

The final step is to evaluate the training materials and presentation the external trainer will use in the classes. The following questions can serve as a checklist:

- Does the speaker use a lot of slides in his or her presentation? Slides can be a problem when students don't have enough light to take notes.
- Does the instructor use transparencies? Have they been prepared professionally? Will the students be given copies of the transparencies?
- Does the speaker make heavy use of chalkboards? Too much chalkboard work usually means too much note taking for the trainees and not enough audiovisual preparation from the speaker.
- Does the speaker use case studies? If he or she does, are the case studies factual? It's best for the company to develop its own case studies and ask the speaker to use those so that the cases will have relevance to the company's business.
- Are role playing and laboratory experiences planned? They can be valuable aids to learning, but they can also limit class size.
- Are homework and required reading a part of the class? If so, can they be completed before the seminar?

Measuring the Return on Investment

The last area of project management training is the determination of the value earned on the dollars invested in training. It is crucial to remember that training shouldn't be performed unless there is a continuous return on dollars for the company. And the speaker's fee is only part of the cost of training. The cost to the company of having employees away from their work during training must be included in the calculation.

Some excellent companies hire outside consultants to determine return on investment. The consultants base their evaluations on personal interviews, on-the-job assessments, and written surveys.

One company tests trainees before and after training to learn how much knowledge the trainees really gained. Another company hires outside consultants to prepare and interpret post training surveys on the value of the specific training received.

The amount of training needed at any one company depends on two factors: whether the company is project driven and whether it has practiced project management long enough to develop a mature project management system. Figure 10-2 shows the amount of project management training offered (including refresher courses) against the number of years in project management. Project-driven organizations offer the most project management training courses, and organizations that have just started implementing project management offer the fewest. That's no surprise. Companies with more than 15 years of experience in applying project management principles show the most variance. (See Figure 1-3, p. 14, again for an explanation of the types of industries.)

Figure 10-2 Amount of training by type of industry and year of project management experience.

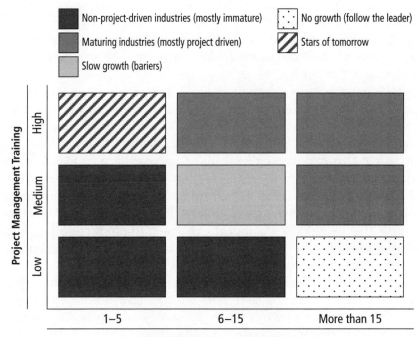

Training and Education at Work

The quality of the project management training and education a company's employees receive is, along with executive buy-in, one of the two most important factors in achieving success and ultimately excellence in project management. Let's look at some case examples of effective training programs.

B. F. Goodrich

The Specialty Chemicals Division of B. F. Goodrich, located in Brecksville, Ohio, is a project-driven operation that has used project management techniques on its capital projects for almost 20 years. By contrast, its parent company is not project driven. The division's projects range from $500,000 to $30 million.

During much of the 20 years the division had been practicing project management, the line managers from the plant had been responsible for project execution. Before 1993, projects frequently ran over budget and missed schedules, because the scopes of projects were poorly defined, project controls and monitoring were weak, staffing was limited, and staff had other priorities.

Additional problems existed in project cost accounting. The format, reporting, and procedures of the cost-tracking system did not allow managers and executives to monitor or control project budgets. For example, international project accounting was reported in a multicurrent format that had no single means of comparing actual spending to budgeted spending.

In 1994, corporate strategy changed and ultimately affected project management. The parent organization (B. F. Goodrich) identified strategic goals that included a significant expansion in production and sales, intended to support a marketing strategy based on the introduction of new products to the marketplace ahead of the competition.

To handle this expansion and growth, it was decided that the organization should be decentralized. This change gave business managers responsibility for their own facilities, resources, and costs. The business managers were two levels above plant managers. Plant managers reported to a manufacturing director for each given product at a given site. The manufacturing director reported to a business manager. It became necessary for the central support organization, including engineering, to become more responsive to the business managers than they had been in the past.

An attempt to decentralize project management had been made in 1993, but numerous problems came up. One set of problems arose because managers had multiple responsibilities at more than one plant in more than one location. Another set of problems resulted from conflicting priorities for line staff when they had project responsibilities.

The pressure to support expansion and to reduce costs led to developing a more sophisticated project management tool. Projects are now outsourced as a single, design–build contract and managed at the central engineering level. A structured process (though relatively informal) has been in place since 1993. The chief engineer today has five experienced project managers available to oversee projects.

The improvements in the design–build project management system at this company have been accelerated primarily through education and training. The education of employees is vital, but just as critical is the training of the contractors and consultants who work with the company. B. F. Goodrich has made it clear to the consultants that such training is a requirement of doing business with the company. The numerous contacts between B. F. Goodrich personnel and outside contractors have resulted in common definitions, risk sharing, and other aspects of the project management process.

Today, the company believes that it has two special areas of strength in project management. The first is its record of success in completing projects on schedule, within budget, and within specification. This allows the company to be responsive to corporate needs. The second strength is the emphasis on the project identification stage of planning. Through both the project authorization and project scope identification stage, basic goals, objectives, and scope of work are carefully defined.

Other strengths include a commitment to accurate budgeting with cost estimating for projects considered a priority. Another strength is the selection of contractors based on their qualifications for each project. The benefits of B. F. Goodrich's commitment to project management are significant and broad. It has been a crucial foundation supporting the successful corporate marketing strategy. The company estimates that project management trims down the cycle time from research and development's initiation of the project to full production to 38 months. Project management also allows improved cost control.

USAA

In Figure 1-3 (p. 14), we saw that insurance companies are usually slow-growth organizations in the area of project management. This is not true of San Antonio-based USAA. Colleen Andreoli, program director for the project management curriculum, describes how training has helped USAA develop its project management system:

> *Background:* In February 1994, a 10-member working group was formed consisting of representatives at the management level from Information Systems (IS) and one Information Technology representative. Over a period of several months, a thorough needs analysis was conducted. The working group received presentations from senior managers, who offered advice on the most important qualities of a project manager. The working group also was briefed by project managers who had led both successful and unsuccessful projects during their careers. They provided input as to what kinds of training would have been helpful to them. These became the foundation for the content of the curricula.
>
> *Evolution of Content and Structure:* Initially, three-levels of curricula for project management were defined based on work experience. Pilots for each level were conducted using IS project managers. An additional pilot was added by request for the business community. At the conclusion of the pilots, student feedback was analyzed and the curriculum was restructured accordingly. Here are the key discoveries.
>
> • All students needed the same core project management skills training. Because the "as-is" culture had only practiced project management by heroics, even experienced project managers were unfamiliar with project management as a formal discipline.

- By eliminating redundancy, the curriculum could be condensed from 11 months to six or eight months, depending on electives selected.

- Combining IS and business partners together in class promoted better communication and understanding between the two communities.

- Some business partners needed a less in-depth curriculum, as they only managed projects occasionally or part-time.

- Excellence in content and delivery was essential. Evaluation forms were completed and analyzed for each class. Only the best of breed classes and vendor providers were retained.

- The price of success is that the demand will exceed the supply. Three course directors are required to administer the program today. Competition for entry in the program is keen.

- To support graduates from the curriculum, awareness level training was needed for project team members and functional managers.

Curriculum Organization Today: The curriculum is organized by a set of common core classes, track-related modules, and electives [see Figure 10-3]. The core classes cover the essential technical and leadership skills related to project management. Track modules cover other areas of specialization such as managing information technology projects, program management, or additional leadership training. Electives include topics such as business process reengineering courses, project management software tool training, a variety of soft-skill modules, or review of the Project Management Body of Knowledge for those pursuing PMP designation.

Figure 10-3 USAA's curriculum for project management

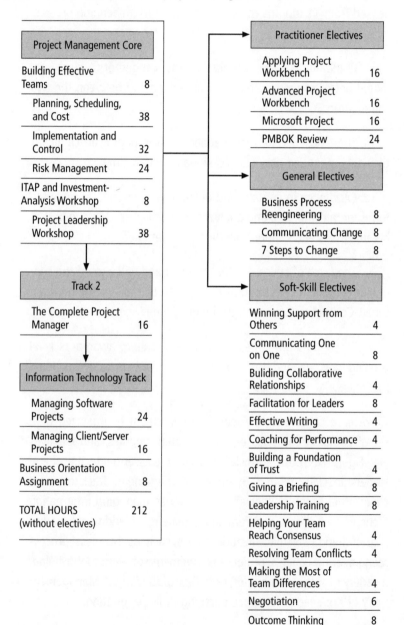

To accommodate their workload, students attend class three to four days out of each month. This approach has proved less of a burden on both the organization and the students. A policy statement is signed by both student and their manager to confirm their understanding of and commitment to the program. Most of the core modules include an exam. Students are required to maintain a running grade average of 80 percent or better. All required classes must be completed to achieve graduate status.

Student Selection: Entry into the curriculum is by nomination. Approximately two months before the start of a curriculum, a call for candidates is issued to senior management. The number of students in each offering is apportioned on a percentage basis across the organization for a total of 24 students per offering.

To kick off each curriculum offering, a welcome party is hosted with the executive sponsor as the guest speaker. At the conclusion of the curriculum, a graduation ceremony is held. Each student is awarded by executive management a certificate honoring their completion of the curriculum and a plaque containing the Project Manager's Professional Code of Ethics. Managers of the students are expected to attend both functions.

Student Placement: All students are required to complete the core modules. Beyond the core are Tracks 1, 2, and 3.

• Track 1 is intended for individuals who have little or no prior project management experience, or experience leading or managing others.

• Track 2 is designed for individuals who have prior project management experience and wish to increase their knowledge in project management as a formal discipline. Track 2 then divides into either the Information Technology Track or the Business Partner Track.

- The audience for Track 3 is individuals already in line management positions who also manage projects and/or other project managers or programs.

Placement in the various tracks is based on several criteria: current position in the organization, experience level determined from a written résumé and personal interview, input from the candidate's manager, a leadership assessment device, and the Skill Gap Analysis Test.

Leadership Assessment: To determine soft-skill training requirements and track placement, students and their managers both complete the leadership assessment. Students will assess themselves; managers will assess the respective students. Results should be reviewed together and, as needed, an appropriate set of soft-skill classes selected to improve the student's leadership skills.

Skill Gap Analysis Test: The test is administered at the start and conclusion of each curriculum for benchmarking purposes. Individual scores are held in confidence. Managers are provided with roll-up averages for the entire group. The questions closely follow the eight areas of the PMI Body of Knowledge. The test's purpose is twofold:

- to gauge student placement

- to measure the student's overall progress.

Perfect scores are not expected; rather, an acceptable range and progress within that range is what is desired. We typically see a 20 to 25 point improvement in student scores.

Mentoring Program: To support the graduates from the curriculum or others who needed project management advice and guidance, consultants were engaged to provide this service. The long-term plan is to develop this ability within USAA.

Awareness Level Series: Also in support of the graduates from the curriculum, three-day classes are offered periodically for project team members and functional managers who provide resources to projects or who manage project managers.

Executive Seminars: A series of two-day executive seminars were offered to educate those in senior management about the discipline of project management.

Informal Project
Management

Over the past 20 years, the most significant change in project management has been the idea that informal project management does work. In the 1950s and 1960s, the aerospace, defense, and large construction industries were the primary users of project management techniques and tools. Because project management was a relatively new management process, customers of the contractors and subcontractors wanted evidence that the system worked. Documentation of the policies and procedures to be used became part of the written proposal. Formal project management, supported by hundreds of policies, procedures, and forms, became the norm. After all, why would a potential customer be willing to sign a $10 million contract for a project to be managed informally?

This chapter clarifies the difference between informal and formal project management, then discusses the four critical elements of informal project management.

Informal versus Formal Project Management

Formal project management has always been expensive. In the early years, the time and resources spent on preparing written policies and procedures had a purpose: They placated the customer. As project management became established, formal documentation was created mostly for the customer. Contractors began managing more informally, while the customer was still paying for formal project management documentation. Table 11-1 shows the major differences between formal and informal project management. As you can see, the most relevant difference is the amount of paperwork.

Table 11-1. Formal versus informal project management.

Factor	Formal Project Management	Informal Project Management
Project manager's level	High	Low to middle
Project manager's authority	Documented	Implied
Paperwork	Exorbitant	Minimal

Paperwork is expensive. Even a routine handout for a team meeting can cost $500 to $2,000 per page to prepare. Executives in excellent companies know that paperwork is expensive. They encourage project teams to communicate without excessive amounts of paper. However, some people are still operating under the mistaken belief that ISO 9000 certification requires massive paperwork.

Figure 11-1 The evolution of policies, procedures, and guidelines.

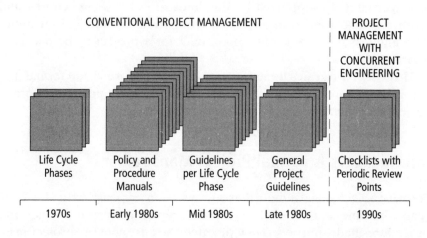

Figure 11-1 shows the changes in paperwork requirements in project management. The early 1980s marked the heyday for lovers of paper documentation. At that time, the average policies and procedures manual probably cost between $3 million and $5 million to prepare initially and $1 million to $2 million to update yearly over the lifetime of the project. Project managers were buried in forms to complete to the extent that they had very little time left for actually managing the projects. Customers began to complain about the high cost of subcontracting, and the paperwork boom started to fade.

Real cost savings didn't materialize until the early 1990s with the growth of concurrent engineering. Concurrent engineering shortened product development times by taking activities that had been done in series and performing them in parallel instead. This change increased the level of risk in each project, which required that project management back away from some of its previous practices. Formal guidelines were replaced by less detailed and more generic checklists.

Policies and procedures represent formality. Checklists represent informality. But informality doesn't eliminate project paperwork altogether. It reduces paperwork requirements to minimally acceptable levels. To move from formality to informality demands a change in organizational culture. (See Figure 11-2.) The four basic elements of an informal culture are these:

- Trust
- Communication
- Cooperation
- Teamwork

Trust

Trusting everyone involved in executing a project is critical. You wake up in the morning, get dressed, and climb into your car to go to work. On a typical morning, you operate the foot pedal for your brakes maybe 50 times. You've never met the people who designed the brakes, manufactured the brakes, or installed the brakes. Yet you still give no thought to whether the brakes will work when you need them. No one broadsides you on the way to work. You don't run over anyone. Then you arrive at work and push the button for the elevator. You've never met the people who designed the elevator, manufactured it, installed it, or inspected it. But again you feel perfectly comfortable riding the elevator up to your floor. By the time you get to your office at 8 a.m., you have trusted your life to uncounted numbers of people whom you've never even met. Still, you sit down in your office and refuse to trust the person in the next office to make a $50 decision.

Figure 11-2 Evolution of paperwork and change of formality levels.

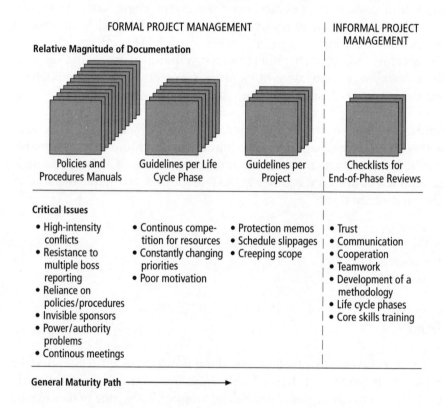

FORMAL PROJECT MANAGEMENT

INFORMAL PROJECT MANAGEMENT

Relative Magnitude of Documentation

| Policies and Procedures Manuals | Guidelines per Life Cycle Phase | Guidelines per Project | Checklists for End-of-Phase Reviews |

Critical Issues

- High-intensity conflicts
- Resistance to multiple boss reporting
- Reliance on policies/procedures
- Invisible sponsors
- Power/authority problems
- Continous meetings

- Continous competition for resources
- Constantly changing priorities
- Poor motivation

- Protection memos
- Schedule slippages
- Creeping scope

- Trust
- Communication
- Cooperation
- Teamwork
- Development of a methodology
- Life cycle phases
- Core skills training

General Maturity Path ⟶

Trust is the key to the successful implementation of informal project management. Without it, project managers and project sponsors would need all that paperwork just to make sure that everyone working on their projects was doing the work just as he or she had been instructed. And trust is also key in building a successful relationship between the contractor/subcontractor and the client. Let's look at an example.

Perhaps the best application of informal project management that I have seen is the Heavy Vehicle Systems Group of Bendix Corporation. Bendix hired a consultant to conduct a three-day training program. The program was custom designed, and during the design phase the consultant asked the vice president and general manager of the division whether he wanted to be trained in formal or informal project management. The vice president opted for informal project management. The reason for his decision? The culture of the division was already based on trust. Line managers were not hired solely based on technical expertise. Hiring and promotions were based on how well the new manager would communicate and cooperate with the other line managers and project managers in making decisions in the best interests of both the company and the project.

When the relationship between a customer and a contractor is based on trust, numerous benefits accrue to both parties. The benefits are apparent in companies such as Hewlett-Packard, Radian International, and various automobile subcontractors. Table 11-2 shows the benefits.

Table 11-2. Benefits of trust in customer-contractor working relationships

Without Trust	With Trust
Continuous competitive bidding	Long-term contracts, repeat business, and sole-source contracts
Massive documentation	Minimal documentation
Excessive customer-contractor team meetings	Minimal number of team meetings
Team meetings with documentation	Team meetings without documentation
Sponsorship at executive levels	Sponsorship at middle-management levels

Communication

In traditional, formal organizations, employees usually claim that communication is poor. Senior managers, however, usually think that communication in their company is just fine. Why the disparity? In most companies, executives are inundated with information communicated to them through frequent meetings and dozens of weekly status reports coming from every functional area of the business. The quality and frequency of information moving down the organizational chart is less consistent, especially in more formal companies. But whether it's a problem with the information flowing up to the executive level or down to the staff, the problem usually originates somewhere upstairs. Senior managers are the usual suspects when it comes to requiring reports and meetings. And many of those reports and meetings are unnecessary and redundant.

Figure 11-3 Internal and external communication channels for project management.

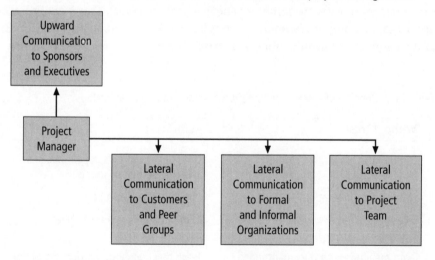

Most project managers prefer to communicate verbally and informally. The cost of formal communication can be high. Project communication includes dispensing information on decisions made, work authorizations, negotiations, and project reports. Project managers in excellent companies believe that they spend as much as 90 percent of their time on internal interpersonal communication with their teams. Figure 11-3 illustrates the communication channels used by a typical project manager. In project-driven organizations, project managers may spend most of their time communicating externally to customers and regulatory agencies.

The two major communication obstacles that must be overcome when a company truly wants to cultivate an informal culture are what I like to call hernia reports and forensic meetings.

Hernia reports result from senior management's belief that that which has not been written has not been said. Although there is some truth to such a belief, the written word comes with a high price tag. We need to consider more than just the time consumed in the preparation of reports and formal memos. There's all the time that recipients spend reading them as well as all the support time taken up in processing, copying, distributing, and filing them.

Status reports written for management are too long if they need a staple or a paper clip. Project reports greater than five or 10 pages often aren't even read. In companies excellent in project management, internal project reports answer three questions as simply as possible:

- Where are we today?
- Where will we end up?
- Are there any problems that require management's involvement?

All of these questions can be answered on one sheet of paper.

Steve Sauer, director of the corporate project management office at BellSouth, points out the reasons for paperwork reduction at BellSouth:

> Further evidence of the evolution of project management at BellSouth is revealed in the areas of project metrics and reporting. BellSouth's officers have requested that standard report formats are developed for projects that focus on the key metrics by which projects should ideally be tracked and measured. This will allow them to review the same information across all projects and facilitate like-for-like comparisons during progress reviews and prioritization sessions.

> The objective of this type of "dashboard" report is to have a standardized, one-page format which focuses on key project deliverables in the areas of cost, schedule, functionality, and quality. This

allows the project to be evaluated based on earned values analysis, which has become widely accepted as a standard of project analysis. The report would also list key items in the areas of risk management, issues management, and change control. Plans are to tie output from the financial reporting systems directly into the project management databases so that status reports can be generated automatically as information is updated.

The second obstacle is the forensic team meeting. A forensic team meeting is a meeting scheduled to last 30 minutes that actually lasts for more than three hours. Forensic meetings are created when senior managers meddle in routine work activities. Even project managers fall into this trap when they present information to management that management should not be dealing with. Such situations are an invitation to disaster.

When it is implemented and used correctly, project management software can reduce the number and length of meetings. For example, the electrical components division of a Fortune 500 company installed project management software to help team members communicate among one another and with managers. Considering just one department within the company, these simple calculations can be made:

- Typical cost per meeting = $550
- Meetings eliminated per week (as a result of using the new software) = 4
- Total annual savings = ($550/meeting) x (4 meetings/week) x (52 weeks/year) = $114,400 per year

When company executives realized the potential cost savings, they looked at the 204 projects within that division that might be submitted for approval over the next two years. Approximately 75 percent of the projects would go through the approval process over the next 18 months. The company executives called for a 50 percent reduction in the number of team meetings necessary to achieve schedule approvals.

- Current average number of meetings required per project schedule approval = 10

- Expected average number after organization begins using project management software = 5
- Average number of attendees per meeting = 10
- Average duration of meetings = 1.25 hours
- Fully burdened labor rate = $70 per hour
- Total annual savings = (204 projects) x (5 meetings/project) x (10 people) x (1.25 hours/meeting) x ($70/hour) = $892,500

Software alone did not save the organization millions of dollars. The company also has a culture based on trust, teamwork, communication, and cooperation. But the company did show that minimizing the number of team meetings can save millions of dollars and improve productivity and efficiency.

Cooperation

Cooperation is the willingness of individuals to work with others for the benefit of all. It includes the voluntary actions of a team working together toward a favorable result. In companies excellent in project management, cooperation is the norm and takes place without the formal intervention of authority. The team members know the right thing to do, and they do it.

In the average company (or the average group of any kind, for that matter), people learn to cooperate as they get to know each other. That takes time, something usually in short supply for project teams. But companies such as Ericsson Telecom AB, the General Motors Powertrain Group, and Hewlett-Packard create cultures that promote cooperation to the benefit of everyone.

Teamwork

Teamwork is the work performed by people acting together with a spirit of cooperation under the limits of coordination. Some people confuse teamwork with morale, but morale has more to do with attitudes toward work than it has to do with the work itself. Obviously, however, good morale is beneficial to teamwork.

In excellent companies, teamwork has these characteristics:

- Employees and managers share ideas with each other and establish high levels of innovation and creativity in work groups.
- Employees and managers trust each other and are loyal to each other and the company.
- Employees and managers are committed to the work they do and the promises they make.
- Employees and managers share information freely.
- Employees and managers are consistently open and honest with each other.

Making people feel that they are part of a team doesn't necessarily require a great deal of effort. Consider the situation at the Engineering and Construction Services Division of Dow Chemical Corporation several years ago. Dow Chemical had requested a trainer to develop a project management training course. The trainer interviewed several of the seminar participants before the training program to identify potential problem areas. The biggest problem appeared to be a lack of teamwork. This shortcoming was particularly evident in the drafting department. The drafting department personnel complained that too many changes were being made to the drawings. They simply couldn't understand the reasons behind all the changes.

The second problem identified, and perhaps the more critical one, was that project managers didn't communicate with the drafting department once the drawings were complete. The drafting people had no idea of the status of the projects they were working on, and they didn't feel as though they were part of the project team.

During the training program, one of the project managers, who was responsible for constructing a large chemical plant, was asked to explain why so many changes were being made to the drawings on his project. He said, "There are three reasons for the changes. First, the customer doesn't always know what they want up front. Second, once we have the preliminary drawings to work with, we build a plastic model of the plant. The model often shows us that equipment needs to be moved for maintenance or safety reasons. Third, sometimes we have to rush into construction well before we have final approval from the Environmental Protection Agency. When the agency finally gives its approval, that approval is often made contingent on making major structural changes to the work already complete." One veteran employee at Dow commented that in his 15 years with the company no one had ever before explained the reasons behind drafting changes.

The solution to the problem of insufficient communication was also easy to repair once it was out in the open. The project managers promised to take monthly snapshots of the progress on building projects and share them with the drafting department. The drafting personnel were delighted and felt more like a part of the project team.

Informal Project Management at Work

Let's review two case studies that illustrate informal project management in action.

Polk Lighting

Polk Lighting (a pseudonym) is a $35 million company located in Jacksonville, Florida. The company manufactures lamps, flashlights, and a variety of other lighting instruments. Its business is entirely based in products and services, and the company doesn't take on contract projects from outside customers. The majority of the company's stock is publicly traded. The president of Polk Lighting has held his position since the company's start-up in 1985.

In 1994, activities at Polk centered on the research and development group, which the president oversaw personally, refusing to hire a research and development director. The president believed in informal management for all aspects of the business, but he had a hidden agenda for wanting to use informal project management. Most companies use informal project management to keep costs down as far as possible. But the president of Polk favored informal project management so that he could maintain control of the research and development group. However, if the company were to grow, the president would need to add more management structure, establish tight project budgets, and possibly make project management more formal than it had been. And the president would probably be forced to hire a research and development director.

Pressure from the company's stockholders eventually forced the president to allow the company to grow. When growth made it necessary for the president to take on heavier administrative duties, he finally hired a vice president of research and development.

Within a few years, the company's sales doubled, but informal project management was still in place. Although budgets and schedules were established as the company grew, the actual management of the projects and the way teams worked together remained informal.

The president learned two important lessons. First, the success of informal project management depends more on the culture of the organization than it does on budgets and schedules. Second, growth does not necessarily destroy an effective informal project management system.

Boeing Aircraft

Boeing was the prime contractor for the U.S. Air Force's new Short-Range Attack Missile (or SRAM) and awarded the subcontract for developing the missile's propulsion system to the Thiokol Corporation.

It's generally assumed that communication between large customers and contractors must be formal because of the potential for distrust when contracts are complex and involve billions of dollars. The use of on-site representatives, however, can change a potentially contentious relationship into one of trust and cooperation when informality is introduced into the relationship.

Two employees from Boeing were carefully chosen to be on-site representatives at the Thiokol Corporation, to supervise the development of the SRAM's propulsion system.

The working relationship between Thiokol's project management office and Boeing's on-site representatives quickly developed into shared trust. Team meetings were held without the exchange of excessive documentation. And each party agreed to cooperate with the other. The Thiokol project manager trusted Boeing's representatives well enough to give them raw data from test results even before Thiokol's engineers could formulate their own opinions on the data. Boeing's representatives in return promised that they wouldn't relay the raw data to Boeing until Thiokol's engineers were ready to share their results with their own executive sponsors.

The Thiokol–Boeing relationship on this project clearly indicates that informal project management can work between customers and contractors. Large construction contractors have had the same positive results in using informal project management and on-site representatives to build trust and cooperation.

Behavioral
Excellence

In the preceding chapter, we saw that companies excellent in project management strongly emphasize training for behavioral skills. In the past, it was thought that project failures were due primarily to poor planning, inaccurate estimating, inefficient scheduling, and lack of cost control. Today, excellent companies realize that project failures have more to do with behavioral shortcomings—poor employee morale, negative human relations, low productivity, and lack of commitment.

This chapter discusses these human factors in the context of situational leadership and conflict resolution. It also provides information on staffing issues in project management, Finally, the chapter offers advice on how to achieve behavioral excellence.

Situational Leadership

As project management has begun to emphasize behavioral management over technical management, situational leadership has also received more attention. The average size of projects has grown, and so has the size of project teams. Process integration and effective interpersonal relations have also taken on more importance as project teams have gotten larger. Project managers now need to be able to talk with many different functions and departments. There's a contemporary project management proverb that goes something like this: "When researcher talks to researcher, there is 100 percent understanding. When researcher talks to manufacturing, there is 50 percent understanding. When researcher talks to sales, there is 0 percent understanding. But the project manager talks to all of them."

Randy Coleman, former senior vice president of the Federal Reserve Bank of Cleveland, emphasizes the importance of tolerance:

> The single most important characteristic necessary in successful project management is tolerance; tolerance of external events and tolerance of people's personalities.... Generally, there are two groups here at the Fed—lifers and drifters. You have to handle the two groups differently but at the same time you have to treat them similarly. You have to bend somewhat for the independents [younger drifters] who have good creative ideas and who you want to keep—those who take risks. You have to acknowledge that you have some trade-offs to deal with.

Many companies start applying project management without understanding the fundamental behavioral differences between project managers and line managers. If we assume that the line manager is not also functioning as the project manager, here are the behavioral differences.

- Project managers have to deal with multiple reporting relationships. Line managers report up a single chain of command.
- Project managers have very little real authority. Line managers hold a great deal of authority by virtue of their titles.
- Project managers often provide no input into employee performance reviews. Line managers provide formal input into the performance reviews of their direct reports.
- Project managers are not always on the management compensation ladder. Line managers always are.
- The project manager's position may be temporary. The line manager's position is permanent.
- Project managers sometimes are at a lower grade level than the project team members. Line managers usually are paid at a higher grade level than their subordinates.

Several years ago, when Ohio Bell was still a subsidiary of American Telephone and Telegraph, a trainer was hired to conduct a three-day course on project management. During the customization process, the trainer was asked to emphasize planning, scheduling, and controlling, and not to bother with the behavioral aspects of project management.

At that time, AT&T offered a course on how to become a line supervisor that all of the seminar participants had already taken. In the discussion that followed between the trainer and the course-content designers, it became apparent that leadership, motivation, and conflict resolution were being taught from a superior-to-subordinate point of view in AT&T's course. When the course-content designers realized from the discussion that project managers provide leadership, motivation, and conflict resolution to employees who do not report directly to them, the trainer was allowed to include project management–related behavioral topics in the seminar.

Organizations must recognize the importance of behavioral factors in working relationships. When they do, they come to understand that project managers should be hired for their overall project management competency, not for their technical knowledge alone. Brian Vannoni, site training manager and principal process engineer at General Electric Plastics, described his organization's approach to selecting project managers:

> The selection process for getting people involved as project managers is based primarily on their behavior skills and skills and abilities as leaders with regard to the other aspects of project management. [With] senior engineers, some of the professional and full-time project managers … take them under their wing, coach and mentor, so that they learn and pick up the other aspects of project management. But the primary skill that we are looking for is, in fact, the leadership skills.

Project managers who have strong behavioral skills are more likely to involve their teams in decision making. And shared decision making is one of the hallmarks of successful project management. Today, project managers are more managers of people than they are managers of technology. According to Robert Hershock, former vice president at 3M:

> The trust, respect, and especially the communications are very, very important. But I think one thing that we have to keep in mind is that a team leader isn't managing technology, he is managing people. If

you manage the people correctly, the people will manage the technology.

In addition, behaviorally oriented project managers are more likely to delegate responsibility to team members than technically strong project managers. Frank Jackson, a senior manager at MCI, thinks:

> … team leaders need to have a focus and a commitment to an ultimate objective. You definitely have to have accountability for your team and the outcome of your team. You've got to be able to share the decision making. You can't single out yourself as the exclusive holder of the right to make decisions. You have got to be able to share that. And lastly again, just to harp on it one more time, is communication. Clear and concise communication throughout the team and both up and down a chain of command is very, very important.

Some organizations prefer to have managers with behavioral expertise act as project managers and have the technical expertise come from a project engineer. Other organizations have found the reverse to be effective. For example, Rose Russett, program coordinator for the General Motors Powertrain Group, described her company's program this way:

> We usually appoint an individual with a technical background as the program manager and an individual with a business and/or systems background as the program administrator. The skills seem to complement one another. The various line managers are ultimately responsible for the technical portions of the program, while the key responsibility of the program manager is to provide the integration of all functional deliverables to achieve the objectives of the program. With that in mind, it helps for the program manager to understand the technical issues, but they add their value not by solving specific technical problems, but by leading the team through a process that will result in the best solutions for the over-

all program, not just for the specific functional area. The program administrator, with input from all team members, develops the program plans, identifies the critical path, and regularly communicates this information to the team throughout the life of the program. This information is used to assist with problem solving, decision making, and risk management.

At the General Motors Powertrain Group, Rose Russett formed a program administrator network to bring together all of the administrators from various programs to create a center of expertise on program management. The network's mission is to

- improve the **management** of the four-phase product development process
- share **lessons learned** across all Powertrain programs
- ensure consistent application of **common** processes and systems required for successful execution of programs
- focus on **process improvement** while project teams focus on successful program execution

Through the program administrator network, and in combination with the highly successful committee sponsorship concept, the General Motors Powertrain Group is positioned for excellence in project management well into the next century. The concept of program administrators, as used by the group, could very well be the future of project management.

Conflict Resolution

Opponents of project management claim that the primary reason why some companies avoid changing over to a project management culture is that they fear the conflicts that inevitably accompany change. Conflicts are a way of life in companies with project management cultures. Conflict can occur on any level of the organization, and conflict is usually the result of conflicting objectives.

The project manager is a conflict manager. In many organizations, the project managers continually fight fires and handle crises arising from interpersonal and interdepartmental conflicts. They are so busy handling conflicts that they delegate the day-to-day responsibility for running their projects to the project teams. Although this arrangement is not the most effective, it is sometimes necessary, especially after organizational restructuring or after a new project demanding new resources has been initiated.

The ability to handle conflicts requires an understanding of why conflicts occur. We can ask four questions, the answers to which are usually helpful in handling, and possibly preventing, conflicts in a project management environment:

- Do the project's objectives conflict with the objectives of other projects currently in development?
- Why do conflicts occur?
- How can we resolve conflicts?
- Is there anything we can do to anticipate and resolve conflicts before they become serious?

Although conflicts are inevitable, they can be planned for. For example, conflicts can easily develop in a team in which the members don't understand each other's roles and responsibilities. Responsibility charts can be drawn to map out graphically who is responsible for doing what on the project. With the ambiguity of roles and responsibilities gone, the conflict is resolved, or future conflict averted.

Resolution means collaboration, and collaboration means that people are willing to rely on each other. Without collaboration, mistrust prevails and progress documentation increases.

The most common types of conflict involve the following:

- Manpower resources
- Equipment and facilities
- Capital expenditures
- Costs
- Technical opinions and trade-offs
- Priorities
- Administrative procedures
- Schedules
- Responsibilities
- Personality clashes

Each of these types of conflict can vary in intensity over the life of the project. The relative intensity can vary as a function of:

- Getting closer to project constraints
- Having only two constraints instead of all three (for example, time and performance but not cost)
- The project life cycle itself
- The individuals who are in conflict

Conflict can be meaningful in that it results in beneficial outcomes. These meaningful conflicts should be allowed to continue as long as project constraints are not violated and beneficial results accrue. An example of a meaningful conflict might be two technical specialists arguing that each has a better way of solving a problem. The beneficial result would be that each tries to find additional information to support his or her hypothesis.

Some conflicts are inevitable and occur over and over again. For example, consider a raw material and finished goods inventory. Manufacturing wants the largest possible inventory of raw materials on hand to avoid possible production shutdowns. Sales and marketing wants the largest finished goods inventory so that the books look favorable and no cash flow problems are possible.

Let's consider five methods that project managers can use to resolve conflicts:

- Confrontation
- Compromise
- Facilitation
- Force
- Withdrawal

Confrontation is probably the most common method used by project managers to resolve conflict. Using confrontation, the project manager faces the conflict directly. With the help of the project manager, the parties in disagreement attempt to persuade one another that their solution to the problem is the most appropriate.

When confrontation doesn't work, the next approach project managers usually try is compromise. In compromise, each of the parties in conflict agrees to trade-offs or makes concessions until a solution is arrived at that everyone involved can live with. This give-and-take approach can easily lead to a win-win solution to the conflict.

The third approach to conflict resolution is facilitation. Using facilitation skills, the project manager emphasizes areas of agreement and de-emphasizes areas of disagreement. For example, suppose that a project manager said, "We've been arguing about five points, and so far we've reached agreement on the first three. There's no reason why we can't agree on the last two points, is there?" Facilitation of a disagreement doesn't resolve the conflict. Facilitation downplays the emotional context in which conflicts occur.

Force is also a method of conflict resolution. A project manager uses force when he or she tries to resolve a disagreement by exerting his or her own opinion at the expense of the other people involved. Often, forcing a solution onto the parties in conflict results in a win-lose outcome. Calling in the project sponsor to resolve a conflict is another form of force project managers sometimes use.

The least-used, and least-effective, mode of conflict resolution is withdrawal. A project director can simply withdraw from the conflict and leave the situation unresolved. When this method is used, the conflict does not go away and is likely to recur later.

Personality conflicts might well be the most difficult conflicts to resolve. Personality conflicts can occur at any time, with anyone, and over anything. And they can seem almost impossible to anticipate and plan for.

Let's look at how one company found a way to anticipate and avoid personality conflicts on one of its projects. Foster Defense Group (a pseudonym) was the government contract branch of a Fortune 500 company. The company understood the potentially detrimental effects of personality clashes on its project teams. But it didn't like the idea of getting the whole team together to air its dirty laundry. The company found a better solution. The project manager put the names of the project team members on a list. Then he interviewed each of the team members one-on-one and asked each to identify the names on the list that he or she had had a personality conflict with in the past. The information remained confidential, and the project manager was able to avoid potential conflicts by separating clashing personalities.

If at all possible, conflict resolution should be handled by the project manager. When the project manager is unable to defuse the conflict, then and only then should the project sponsor be brought in to help solve the problem. Even then, the sponsor should not come in and force a resolution to the conflict. Instead, the sponsor should facilitate further discussion between the project managers and the team members in conflict.

Staffing for Excellence

Project manager selection is always an executive-level decision. In excellent companies, however, executives go beyond simply selecting the project manager. They use the selection process to accomplish the following:

- Project managers are brought on board early in the life of the project to assist in outlining the project, setting its objectives, and even planning for marketing and sales. The project manager's role in customer relations becomes increasingly important.
- Executives assign project managers for the life of the project and project termination. Sponsorship can change over the life cycle of the project, but not the project manager.
- Project management is given its own career ladder.
- Project managers given a role in customer relations are also expected to help sell future project management services long before the current project is complete.
- Executives realize that project scope changes are inevitable. The project manager is viewed as a manager of change.

Companies excellent in project management are prepared for crises. Both the project manager and the line managers are encouraged to bring problems to the surface as quickly as possible so that there is time for contingency planning and problem solving. Replacing the project manager is no longer the first solution for problems on a project. Project managers are replaced only when they try to bury problems.

A defense contractor was behind schedule on a project, and the manufacturing team was asked to work extensive overtime to catch up. Two of the manufacturing people, both union employees, used the wrong lot of raw materials to produce a $65,000 piece of equipment needed for the project. The customer was unhappy because of the missed schedules and cost overruns that resulted from having to replace the useless equipment. An inquisitionlike meeting was convened and attended by senior executives from both the customer and the contractor, the project manager, and the two manufacturing employees. When the customer's representative asked for an explanation of what had happened, the project manager stood up and said, "I take full responsibility for what happened. Expecting people to work extensive overtime leads to mistakes. I should have been more careful." The meeting was adjourned with no one being blamed. When word spread through the company about what the project manager did to protect the two union employees, everyone pitched in to get the project on schedule, even working uncompensated overtime.

Human behavior is also a consideration in assigning staff to project teams. Team members should not be assigned to a project solely on the basis of technical knowledge. It has to be recognized that some people simply can't work effectively in a team environment. For example, the director of research and development at a New England company had an employee, a 50-year-old engineer, who held two master's degrees in engineering disciplines. He had worked for the previous 20 years on one-person projects. The director reluctantly assigned the engineer to a project team. After years of working alone, the engineer trusted no one's results but his own. He refused to work cooperatively with the other members of the team. He even went so far as redoing all the calculations passed on to him from other engineers on the team.

To solve the problem, the director reassigned the engineer to another project on which he supervised two other engineers with less experience. Again, the older engineer tried to do all of the work himself, even if it meant overtime for him and no work for the others.

Ultimately, the director had to admit that some people are not able to work cooperatively on team projects. The director went back to assigning the engineer to one-person projects on which the engineer's technical abilities would be useful.

Robert Hershock, former vice president at 3M, once observed:

> There are certain people who you just don't want to put on teams. They are not team players, and they will be disruptive on teams. I think that we have to recognize that and make sure that those people are not part of a team or team members. If you need their expertise, you can bring them in as a consultant to the team but you never, never put people like that on the team.

I think the other thing is that I would never, ever eliminate the possibility of anyone being a team member no matter what the management level is. I think if they are properly trained, these people at any level can be a participator in the team concept.

Frank Jackson, a senior manager at MCI, believes that it is possible to find a team where any individual can contribute:

People should not be singled out as not being team players. Everyone has got the ability to be on a team and to contribute to a team based on the skills and the personal experiences that they have had. If you move into the team environment, one other thing that is very important is that you not hinder communication. Communication is the key to the success of any team and any objective that a team tries to achieve.

One of the critical arguments still being waged in the project management community is whether an employee (even a project manager) should have the right to refuse an assignment. At Minnesota Power and Light, an open project manager position was posted, but nobody applied for the job. The company recognized that the employees probably didn't understand what the position's responsibilities were. After more than 80 people were trained in the fundamentals of project management, there were numerous applicants for the open position.

It's the kiss of death to assign someone to a project manager's job if that person is not dedicated to the project management process and the accountability it demands.

Keys to Behavioral Excellence

There are some distinguishing actions that project managers can take to ensure the successful completion of their projects. These include:

- Insisting on the right to select the key project team
- Negotiating for key team members with proven track records in their fields

- Developing commitment and a sense of mission from the outset
- Seeking sufficient authority from the sponsor
- Coordinating and maintaining a good relationship with the client, parent, and team
- Seeking to enhance the public's opinion of the project
- Having key team members assist in decision making and problem solving
- Developing realistic budgets, schedules, and performance estimates and goals
- Maintaining backup strategies (contingency plans) in anticipation of potential problems
- Providing a team structure that is appropriate and yet flexible and flat
- Going beyond formal authority to maximize their influence over people and key decisions
- Employing a workable set of project planning and control tools
- Avoiding overreliance on any one type of control tool
- Stressing the importance of meeting cost, schedule, and performance goals
- Giving priority to achieving the mission or function of the project
- Keeping changes under control
- Seeking ways to assure job security for effective project team members

Earlier in this book, I claimed that a project cannot be successful unless it is recognized as a project and gains the support of top-level management. Top-level management must be willing to commit company resources and provide the necessary administrative support so that the project becomes part of the company's day-to-day routine of doing business. In addition, the parent organization must develop an atmosphere conducive to good working relationships among the project manager, parent organization, and client organization.

There are actions that ensure that the organization as a whole supports individual projects and project teams as well as the overall project management system:

- Showing a willingness to coordinate efforts
- Demonstrating a willingness to maintain structural flexibility
- Showing a willingness to adapt to change

- Performing effective strategic planning
- Maintaining rapport
- Putting proper emphasis on past experience
- Providing external buffering
- Communicating promptly and accurately
- Exhibiting enthusiasm
- Recognizing that projects do, in fact, contribute to the capabilities of the whole company

Executive sponsors can take the following actions to make project success more likely:

- Selecting a project manager at an early point in the project who has a proven track record in behavioral skills and technical skills
- Developing clear and workable guidelines for the project manager
- Delegating sufficient authority to the project manager so that he or she can make decisions in conjunction with the project team members
- Demonstrating enthusiasm for and a commitment to the project and the project team
- Developing and maintaining short and informal lines of communication
- Avoiding excessive pressure on the project manager to win contracts
- Avoiding arbitrarily slashing or ballooning the project team's cost estimates
- Avoiding buy-ins
- Developing close, not meddlesome, working relationships with the principal client contact and project manager

The client organization can exert a great deal of influence on the behavioral aspects of a project by minimizing team meetings, rapidly responding to requests for information, and simply allowing the contractor to conduct business without interference. The positive actions of client organizations also include:

- Showing a willingness to coordinate efforts
- Maintaining rapport
- Establishing reasonable and specific goals and criteria for success
- Establishing procedures for making changes

- Communicating promptly and accurately
- Committing client resources as needed
- Minimizing red tape
- Providing sufficient authority to the client's representative, especially in decision making

With these actions as the basic foundation, it should be possible to achieve behavioral success, which includes:

- Encouraging openness and honesty from the start from all participants
- Creating an atmosphere that encourages healthy competition, but not cutthroat competition or liars' contests
- Planning for adequate funding to complete the entire project
- Developing a clear understanding of the relative importance of cost, schedule, and technical performance goals
- Developing short and informal lines of communication and a flat organizational structure
- Delegating sufficient authority to the principal client contact and allowing prompt approval or rejections of important project decisions
- Rejecting cost buy-ins
- Making prompt decisions regarding contract okays or go-aheads
- Developing close working relationships with project participants
- Avoiding arm's-length relationships
- Avoiding excessive reporting schemes
- Making prompt decisions on changes

Companies that are excellent in project management have gone beyond the standard actions as listed previously. These additional actions for excellence include the following:

- The outstanding project manager has these demonstrable qualities.
  —Understands and demonstrates competency as a project manager
  — Works creatively and innovatively in a nontraditional sense only when necessary; does not look for trouble
  — Demonstrates high levels of self-motivation from the start
  — Has a high level of integrity; goes above and beyond politics and gamesmanship
  — Is dedicated to the company and not just the project; is never self-serving

— Demonstrates humility in leadership
— Demonstrates strong behavioral integration skills both internally and externally
— Thinks proactively rather than reactively
— Is willing to assume a great deal of risk and will spend the appropriate time needed to prepare contingency plans
— Knows when to handle complexity and when to cut through it; demonstrates tenaciousness and perseverance
— Is willing to help people realize their full potential; tries to bring out the best in people
— Communicates in a timely manner and with confidence rather than despair

• The project manager maintains high standards of performance for self and team.
— Stresses managerial, operational, and product integrity
— Conforms to moral codes and acts ethically in dealing with people internally and externally
— Never withholds information
— Is quality conscious and cost conscious
— Discourages politics and gamesmanship; stresses justice and equity
— Strives for continuous improvement but in a cost-conscious manner

• The outstanding project manager organizes and executes the project in a sound and efficient manner.
— Informs employees at the project kickoff meeting how they will be evaluated
— Prefers a flat project organizational structure over a bureaucratic one
— Develops a project process for handling crises and emergencies quickly and effectively
— Keeps the project team informed in a timely manner
— Does not require excessive reporting; creates an atmosphere of trust
— Defines roles, responsibilities, and accountabilities up front
— Establishes a change management process that involves the customer

• The outstanding project manager knows how to motivate.

—Always uses two-way communication

—Is empathetic with the team and a good listener

—Involves team members in decision making; always seeks ideas and solutions; never judges an employee's idea hastily

—Never dictates

—Gives credit where credit is due

—Provides constructive criticism rather than making personal attacks

—Publicly acknowledges credit when credit is due but delivers criticism privately

—Makes sure that team members know that they will be held accountable and responsible for their assignments

—Always maintains an open-door policy; is readily accessible, even for employees with personal problems

—Takes action quickly on employee grievances; is sensitive to employees' feelings and opinions

—Allows employees to meet the customers

—Tries to determine each team member's capabilities and aspirations; always looks for a good match; is concerned about what happens to the employees when the project is over

—Tries to act as a buffer between the team and administrative/ operational problems

• The project manager is ultimately responsible for turning the team into a cohesive and productive group for an open and creative environment.

—The team demonstrates innovation.

—The team exchanges information freely.

—The team is willing to accept risk and invest in new ideas.

—The team is provided with the necessary tools and processes to execute the project.

—The team dares to be different; it is not satisfied with simply meeting the competition.

—The team understands the business and the economics of the project.

—The team tries to make sound business decisions rather than just project decisions.

Rising Stars and
Future Directions

Some companies are simply complacent, doing what they've done and maintaining their market share, no matter how small. Other companies, however, aren't satisfied with the status quo. They want to exceed their customers' expectations and not just meet them. Such companies thrive on continuous improvement in everything they do. Their cultures are second to none. And what's truly amazing is that companies such as Nortel, Motorola, Radian International, United Technologies Automotive, Johnson Controls, and Roadway Express have accomplished their excellence in project management in less than five years. This chapter looks at these stars of the present and the future.

United Technologies Automotive

One company that is well positioned for the next century has been continuously climbing the ladder to excellence. United Technologies Automotive, a subsidiary of United Technologies Corporation, in Dearborn, Michigan, produces wiring systems for auto makers. Almost all of its projects are internal and are valued at $10,000 to $400 million. The wiring systems division initiated project management for the company, with the goal of developing and implementing a project management system for product development and launch.

D. William Pumphrey, vice president for Chrysler Programs at UT Automotive, explained how program management developed:

> Program management started at UT Automotive wiring systems division with PMs reporting to the sales department and using assigned resources from the functional departments. UT

Automotive followed a loosely defined process of product development, which included quarterly management reporting. In the next phase, we co-located the teams, putting all functional resources assigned to the team within the same area, along with the PM. The next phase was to develop a matrix organization as described below.

Other divisions within UT Automotive are in different stages of project management maturity, varying in part due to the size and complexity of the product programs for which they were developed. In order to develop common processes and practices, a single product development and launch process (PDLP) was developed. In essence, this PDLP represents a complex work breakdown structure to be followed by each program within UT Automotive. With the different uses of project management within UT Automotive, we are at different stages of implementation of the PDLP within the company.

Asked what UT Automotive does very well in project management, Pumphrey said:

UT Automotive's greatest strength in project management is its matrix organizational structure used within its wiring systems division. Given the size and complexity of its programs, UT Automotive has the ability to staff dedicated program teams. In the matrix organization, both the program managers and the functional managers report to a single executive responsible for the product development team (PDT). Each PDT at UT Automotive handles between four and eight programs, each having its own dedicated (some cases use shared resources) team and program manager. The program teams are established at the beginning of the program, and resources are assigned primarily by the functional manager based upon the task required. Each functional area has an assigned "node leader" who has a direct reporting relationship to both the program manager and the functional manager. This is made effective because the PM and FM both have shared objectives. Any disagreement in the interpretation or fulfillment of these objectives can be quickly resolved with the executive of the PDT to whom both the PM and the FM also directly report.

UT Automotive's co-located teams put all functional team resources and the PM within the same office environment. Plant (manufacturing) resources are made easily available with state-of-the-art videoconferencing and electronic mail systems. This provides ease of communication and stronger teamwork within the long-term programs which we manage. Issues are resolved quickly, concurrent design is facilitated, and continuous improvement opportunities are more readily identified.

Best practices are developed and shared with the teams from "Centers of Excellence." These COEs concentrate on advanced work and support activities to the development and production programs within the company.

This has created a strong team relationship, focused objectives, and ease of conflict resolution. The result has been successful programs on time, within budget, within specification, and meeting customer satisfaction.

In high-pressure markets, executives must predict the future accurately and plan for it. Asked what the future holds for project management at UT Automotive and the auto industry in general, Pumphrey replied:

UT Automotive will continue to expand its project management capability throughout its company, concentrating on the incorporation of our PDLP. But we will also begin to concentrate on improved scope management. Improved scope management is critical for the automotive industry and an area in which UT Automotive sees an opportunity for competitive differentiation.

The auto industry is known for its quest for faster "time to market." Reacting to marketplace changes in this industry is not measured in days or weeks but rather months and years. As a result, original equipment manufacturers (OEMs) are well known for bringing change to vehicle programs throughout the development period, especially prior to and immediately after product launch. Reasons for changes include cost, content, volume or product specification changes. Without shared scope management, suppliers are left choosing between accepting significantly increased risk associated with change incorporation or the risk of lost business from refusing to comply. The former nearly always prevails, adding significant cost to the system either through crashing projects, poor quality, decreased reliability or resulting customer dissatisfaction. Managing scope between the OEM customer and the supplier team can result in improved performance of both partners through better risk assessment and, therefore, improved decision making.

UT Automotive is moving toward the formal establishment of scope definition and the shared management of its development with the OEM customers. As change has threatened, the scope change team can analyze the impact to timing, cost, specification, and satisfaction. Change decisions then become joint, with both parties understanding the associated risk. We do not expect this to be an easy task since change will be required. However, we expect the management of this change to be greatly improved.

UT Automotive is also in a unique position to take program management into systems integration whereby our company's role as a tier one supplier expands to include entire subsystems, or modules. We manufacture vehicle interiors, electrical and electronic systems which can be combined in design, manufacture, and assembly to derive greater cost efficiencies. In these cases, project management is paramount to success, since we now must manage several concurrent development projects and subsuppliers. Common project management practices, procedures, and styles will become key to the coordination of these diverse groups of people and organizations. Success in systems integration provides significant opportunity for UT Automotive to provide unique competitive advantages to our customers. Project management will be critical to exploiting these opportunities.

Pumphrey's comments embody the essence of excellence. Simply stated, the project management culture at UT Automotive includes:

- A standardized methodology that includes integration of risk management, project management, concurrent engineering, scope management changes, and customer management
- Effective communication
- Co-located teams
- Training and education programs
- Effective customer relations

UT Automotive's culture evolved in only four years. Robert V. Sweeney, manager, Program Management Office, described the evolution of project management at UT Automotive:

From the 1970s through the 1990s, UT Automotive grew, in large part, by acquisitions of other related organizations. By the 1990s, UT Automotive had four main business units, with sales over $2 billion per year. The four business units had the potential to supply a car company with any component or system on the interior of a vehicle, with the exception of seats and carpeting. The four business units were wiring systems, which made wiring harnesses and associated components; interiors, which made instrument panels, interior door panels, headliners, and steering wheels; input controls, which made switches, keyless remotes, and instrument clusters; and motor systems, which made the small motors that power door windows, latches, antennas, and headlights.

Although UT Automotive had the capability to supply systems orga-
nizationally, it was generally incapable managerially. Through three
changes in leadership in the late 1980s and early 1990s, the need
for a culture shift was recognized. The growth accomplished
through acquisitions resulted in an organization with four business
units and dozens of identities. The business units were left to define
for themselves how they could manage their business. Program
management and project management both were held in disdain.

In February 1995, the president commissioned a team of representatives from across the business units, headquarters, and European
operations. The team's mission was to obtain direct feedback from
customers on UT Automotive's strengths and weaknesses, obtain
similar information from internal stakeholders, and benchmark
other companies' project management methods, techniques, and
processes. The team presented its analyses and made its recommendations to the president in May 1995.

In June 1995, the team was asked to develop a common product
development process to be used by all of the business units. The
foundation of the process was built on the Automotive Industry
Action Group's Advanced Product Quality Planning process. This
process was compared to the team's findings in benchmarked companies. Specifically, UT Automotive and other businesses contributed to the development of this process: Pratt & Whitney, Pratt
& Whitney of Canada, Otis Elevators, Carrier, Sikorsky, and Hamilton
Standard. The process guidelines include tools for addressing the
use of project management, the role of the program/project manager, and the function and organization of cross-functional program
teams.

During the summer of 1995, a draft of the process was published
and sent out to 300 stakeholders in UT Automotive. The feedback
resulted in more than 800 changes to the draft. The president was

impressed enough with the effort that he moved the roll-out date to his direct reports from 12/15/95 to 11/8/95.

On November 8, 1995, the president and his direct reports from around the world attended one of two half-day overviews of UT Automotive's Product Development and Launch Process. The president impressed on his executives that use and adherence to the process was the only option. One general manager expressed concern that the process had not been pilot tested. He asked the president, "So, you expect us to take this book and metaphorically jump off the cliff and figure out how to fly before we hit the bottom?" After a few moments of thought, the president answered, "Yes."

Motorola

The concept of continuous improvement is critical to those companies that are excellent in project management. According to Martin O'Sullivan, vice president and director of business process management at Motorola:

Motorola is constantly striving to improve our processes. What worked well last year, or this year, may not meet our needs in the future. We have goals to improve the effectiveness of project performance and product development. We believe that how effectively we implement the program management process is a key to achieving our goal. We intend to be the best in class at program management and are investing resources to this end.

Radian International

Radian International has one of the best cultures for project management around. The project-driven, medium-size company specializes in providing consulting services in project management and technical issues. William E. Corbett, senior vice president at Radian, believes that there were two significant events that forced Radian to become a mature project management organization:

- The decision to emphasize client-focused, value-added services rather than technical skills maintenance and management.
- The decision to flatten and de-layer our line management organization to lower our costs which necessarily shifted much of the burden and responsibility for managing our business to our project managers.

To accomplish those goals, Radian developed a training and education program and a project management system that is very responsive to customer feedback. When some people are asked how long it took their companies to reach maturity in project management, they respond that it took one or two years, and they cite a definitive time period. William Corbett answered this way:

> On the one hand, I would say 20 years. On the other, I'm not sure we are there yet. I can still see clear needs for improvement, and our systems continue to evolve. We have mature training programs, well-established lines of accountability and responsibility, reward/ evaluation systems linked to project performance, and a standard project management methodology (as documented in our project quality specification [PQS]). We need more training and new systems (e.g., standard software) to support our earned value planning and tracking and our risk management and performance auditing processes.

The following activities were put in place at Radian to accelerate the maturity process:

> - We established our PQS process to document our methodology for achieving excellence on every project (what it is; how to do it). Our process emphasizes planning, client involvement, timely communications, regular status reviews, team work, employee empowerment and peer review of project plans, methods, and deliverables.

- We formalized a project management training program utilizing the best of what we could find in the way of training resources from both internal and external sources.

- We select project managers who are trained and who have the requisite skills (not by seniority, etc.).

- We get customer feedback on our work and share that feedback with our project teams.

Radian has realized tangible benefits as the result of excellence in project management. The benefits include:

- Increased commitment of our project managers to the success of our business

- Happier clients/more repeat business

- Increased staff involvement in and focus upon serving our clients rather than focusing on internal issues

- Reduced overruns/writeoffs

Battelle Memorial Institute

Another organization that has become a rising star in project management is the Pacific Northwest National Laboratory (PNNL), in Richland, Washington, operated by the Battelle Memorial Institute for the U.S. Department of Energy. The project management discipline has been recognized as important by the laboratory and its primary customers for years. On large multidisciplinary projects, project management concepts have been applied for about 10 or 15 years. On smaller traditional research projects, project management is being introduced gradually. The William R. Wiley Environmental Molecular Sciences Laboratory Project, a $230 million facility construction and equipment acquisition effort funded by the Department of Energy and managed by Battelle staff, was a significant driver that forced the Pacific Northwest National Laboratory to improve its project management practices.

The Environmental Molecular Sciences Laboratory was chartered as a Department of Energy line-item project in 1989. The Pacific Northwest National Library formally endorsed project management concepts in a professional sense to enable delivery of the Environmental Molecular Sciences Laboratory scope, and the application of project management concepts was expanded to a new Battelle–wide business model that is currently being implemented. Before 1989, the Pacific Northwest National Laboratory used an informal project management process to deliver approximately 1,000 projects per year. The projects were undertaken within the laboratory's major research programs.

In the new Battelle business model, the basic business unit is the research project. Traditionally, Battelle performs projects that range from basic scientific research to enhanced engineering activities. Projects with a basic science orientation generally are funded by grants, with very little project management discipline required by the customer. These projects typically are funded for less than $100,000. Larger, multidisciplinary projects, where coordination and collaboration are necessary, usually have a greater application of project management discipline. As the marketplace has driven more accountability for adherence to scope, schedule, and budget, project management concepts have begun to play a more important role in the Pacific Northwest National Laboratory's management activities.

Before 1989, the Pacific Northwest National Laboratory was an inconsistent project management practitioner on large projects. It could deliver the smaller $50,000 to $100,000 projects with regularity, but the larger projects were frequently over budget and/or late. The Pacific Northwest National Laboratory consistently scored high marks technically, but lost credibility and, therefore, opportunity due to poor baseline project performance. The opportunity to deliver the Environmental Molecular Sciences Laboratory in 1989 improved the Pacific Northwest National Laboratory's project management focus. Professional project managers were hired to deliver the Environmental Molecular Sciences Laboratory scope, and the skill set brought by those managers has spread and continues to grow in effectiveness and application within the research environment. Over the last seven years, the Pacific Northwest National Laboratory has made improving its project management systems a high priority, and the momentum of this effort continues. Maturity in an individual project can be achieved quickly. However, it takes many years of new systems and requirements to become accepted and routinely used for the full value of the changes to be realized.

Asked what the Pacific Northwest National Laboratory did to drive the maturity process forward, key project management practitioners said:

- "Clarified roles, responsibilities, accountabilities, and authorities of line and project managers"
- "Published and widely distributed the project management requirements of our customer(s)"
- "Implemented a work-plan authorization process for major task elements that are derived from the project WBS"

The Pacific Northwest National Laboratory now performs the following elements of project management very well:

- "Project management application in the research environment which blends the need for research flexibility with project management control"
- "Integrated project scheduling and earned value management on large projects"
- "Extended project management principles into the operations environment as part of the maturity process, the Battelle business model, and the future of PNNL and Battelle."

Battelle and the Pacific Northwest National Laboratory have achieved these benefits:

- "Five-year noncompetitive extensions of the operating contract for PNNL based primarily on outstanding performance"
- "Better 'on-time' and 'on-budget' delivery of contracted work"
- "Improved credibility re: project management decisions = competitive edge"
- "Better ability to define the cost of a project and, therefore, make rational decisions about descoping or impacts due to change = better cost control and customer interaction"

Project managers at the Pacific Northwest National Laboratory have a vision of the changes they expect to see during the next 10 years:

The national laboratory system is facing tremendous challenges. The lab system must (1) deal with significantly reduced federal research budgets, (2) define a distinctive mission or capability for each lab, and (3) integrate distinctive capabilities or skills within individual labs or among several labs to solve larger problems facing DOE and the nation. The application of established project management principles in managing complex, integrated projects and laboratory operations can help us to effectively meet these challenges and make a real contribution to the success of PNNL. We also expect to see:

- More informality in the project management career path

- More formal qualification requirements for project managers

- Enhanced and broader support specialists and systems

- Greater use of information from clients as the basis for continuously improving performance

OEC Medical Systems

OEC Medical Systems of Salt Lake City, Utah, a small manufacturer of medical equipment, has accepted the challenge to achieve excellence in project management. John Benson, a senior program manager at OEC, described the driving forces behind project management in his company:

About five years ago, one major project in the company needed focal points for all company activity. A project manager was appointed to each of two major subcomponents which would be integrated and tested together at the end. This was a $7 million, two-plus–yearlong project. Project management was necessary to coordinate all the complexities and to focus company/project communication upward and downward. Additionally, the company had to establish much more stringent documentation, development, and testing processes in order to comply with FDA medical device safety requirements.

According to Benson, there were three significant events:

- FDA and other national and international medical device safety regulations require a documented development process which in turn lends itself directly to structured project management.

- The need to reduce our time to market in the face of increasing competition and increasing pressure on health care costs in the industry.

- A need to improve product quality by decreasing repairs, reducing machine downtime, improving feature/performance quality over the competition, and to reduce and ultimately eliminate mandatory field retrofit situations.

It took about two years to start bringing projects in on time. It has taken one to two more to establish change control processes. Our company has not yet committed all functional areas of the company to project management training. We are struggling to improve in that area and to formally enhance TQM and continuous improvement by training people in the company.

Some companies find it difficult to quantify the benefits of excellence in project management. Fortunately, OEC Medical Systems has been able to quantify benefits. According to Benson:

- Projects tend to meet schedule and cost targets and reach the market faster than previously.

- Fewer surprises to upper management or the teams.

- Improved product quality: OEC has seen a 27 percent decrease in the number of service calls for "hard failures" in the first 12 months of our current product over previous products and a 44 percent decrease in the number of service calls in the first 24 months of product life.

- Products are reaching "maturity" 50 percent faster than previously based on reliability life cycle curves, and product warranty costs are decreasing.

Benson described what OEC Medical Systems sees as the future of its project management program:

Project management has proved itself to OEC. It will continue to become ingrained into the culture as a way of life here. It will be the platform for promoting company performance through the adoption of continuous improvement philosophies such as TQM, risk management, concurrent engineering, design for manufacturing, and continuous flow manufacturing. Project management and the team approach are fast becoming the backbone of OEC product development.

Johnson Controls

Any list of the stars of tomorrow in project management must include the Automotive Systems Group of Johnson Controls. Earlier in the book, we looked at how the Plymouth, Michigan, company grew by integrating project management with TQM and concurrent engineering. Richard J. Crayne, manager of engineering operations in the Automotive Systems Group, provided a chronology of how the company achieved excellence in project management:

We have used project management for manufacturing start-ups on "white-box" programs for over 12 years. As we have grown into a full-service, Tier 1 supplier, we have integrated PM with our Total Quality Controland Simultaneous Development Team methodology. We have been using PM intensely for over 10 years.

We needed tools to help us meet aggressive timing requirements on product development projects. We could not be late for program milestones. We developed a phased approach with gateways that we still use today.

We gained responsibility for management of complete seat programs from initial concepts to production, including supply-base management and sourcing decisions. At the time, most projects included building a new plant and launching all new products. As we were working toward using SDT methods, we knew that we needed a structured framework for all projects.

We brought the process to maturity as part of developing our divisionwide TQC system. This took about one year to develop and two years to incorporate into all projects. The process continued in the engineering areas where we added two more levels of subprojects. We are applying this approach now to our manufacturing areas to build a multiproject program management system.

We appointed a TQC director and a director of program management. Their duties included developing and implementing a mature process. Additional levels were added after we formed a Project Office for Engineering. This group now develops, implements, and supports several software tools for quoting, creating timelines, and document control. We developed and implemented a comprehensive training program to support SDTs in the use of these tools and other aspects of PM.

We excel at managing timing and overcoming timing crisis situations due to our customers' focus on meeting milestone commitments. We are now controlling project costs via our custom quoting software. We are improving our quality of execution by standardizing and auditing our key subprocesses. We are applying this expertise toward development of quotation packages for seat system proposals to acquire new business.

Excellent companies recognize the need for continuous improvement. Crayne believes that the following improvements will occur over the next several years at Johnson Controls:

> We are integrating our systems for PM, project data management, product change, and core technology use. We are integrating our top-to-bottom levels for PM, engineering, and manufacturing to better monitor and manage these relationships and impacts. We are working toward resource requirements and leveling at the task level across multiple levels and disciplines.

The benefits at Johnson Controls include:

> We have reduced our product development time and improved our ability to maintain our "best methods" for many customers' timing requirements. We have increased our customers' confidence in our ability to deliver. We are using these systems as part of our "solution provider" approach. By controlling our processes, we are in a much better position to do proper value analysis & value engineering analysis at the right times. Future integration of our new product development process is expected to yield large project and product cost reductions.

Lessons Learned

Before the 1990s, companies handled lessons learned through team debriefings. That approach limits the lessons learned to the people on the project team. One company achieved tremendous success on a project. The division had made improvements to the manufacturing process that shortened product development time. To spread the new process to other divisions, the project team was disbanded, and the team members were assigned to other divisions. But somehow the team members' new knowledge was not transplanted to the sister divisions. The vice president then reconvened the team and asked them to write a lessons-learned case study that included seed questions and a teacher's guide on how to use the case study. The case study then became required reading in almost all training programs. Finally, the word about the manufacturing changes spread quickly.

There are two ways to learn: from successes (let's hope they're yours) and failures (let's pray they're someone else's). Both ways provide valuable information. Some people contend that knowledge learned from failure may be more valuable than knowledge learned from success. Other people contend, however, that learning to do the right things right the first time (success) is the way to go. But documented lessons-learned case studies will likely be emphasized in the future. Each project team will be required to prepare a documented lessons-learned case study that will then be used by training personnel.

Not all companies favor the idea of preparing case studies, especially on project failure. These companies make two points: (1) no one is going to want to prepare a case study highlighting their own mistakes and then sign off on it. (2) Even if the case study were disguised, colleagues would know who worked on the project. For documented lessons-learned case studies to be effective, senior managers must avoid promoting the idea that there's someone to blame for every mistake.

Lessons learned can also apply to the senior levels of management. Senior managers are, and always will be, the architects of corporate cultures. Steve Gregerson, vice president at the BTR Sealing Systems Group, in Madison Heights, Michigan, was asked three questions to gain his extensive experience in project/program management:

- What did you do at your previous employer to create excellence in project management?
- What lessons were learned in evolving this system of excellence in program management?
- What are you now planning to do at BTR Sealing to accelerate project management maturity and excellence?

In response to the first question, Gregerson described four activities that led to excellence in project management:

- Customer focused, co-located teams: Teams were established which had complete responsibility for all aspects of satisfying customer requirements and gaining new business. These teams were linked via a solid line reporting structure which connected all of the appropriate company activities. They were also loosely matrixed with "Centers for Excellence," which had the responsibility to develop and implement best practices across the teams. I evolved these teams into "Global Network Teams," which are virtually co-located as customer requirements required multiple country partic-ipation.

• Program office and program planners: As the need for more cumbersome program management techniques became apparent, I recognized the need to both develop these techniques within our company and to give the program managers relief from the dedi-cated tasks of program planning and tracking. The establishment of a program office, linked via a matrixed solid-line relationship to each team program planner allowed a mechanism to develop con-sistent program management practices in the teams, while shifting many of the technical aspects to the program planner.

• Team quality operating system metrics: The teams developed a set of about 20 key metrics, which were linked to our customer satisfaction objectives. This system complied with standard QOS approaches and provided a way to improve team focus, awareness and improvements in its performance.

• Gateway process: A basic sequencing of "the right way" of developing new products was developed and published as a prod-uct development and launch manual for the company. It was basi-cally modeled after the automotive industry's Action Group Advanced Products Quality Planning process. We also created eight gateways each team needed to pass through in order to proceed with management blessing. We then used Microsoft Project to cre-ate the ideal model for sequencing a program including events, deliverables, relationships, durations, responsibilities, etc. These master models then served as the starting point for program plans within all the teams.

Regardless of how great the final results look, lessons are always learned along the way, according to Gregerson:

- There was too much focus on compliance, not enough on value-added activity: We did move the organization into doing more, earlier. A lessons learned was that we also needed to improve the value of accomplishing a given deliverable. Example: Process Failure Mode and Effects Analysis (PFMEA).

- The plan was great until the customer blew it apart: Great focus was put on doing things the right way. This worked well as long as the plan was somewhat on track. What occurred too often was a significant program change (timing, design, scope, etc.) that was not within our capabilities to respond to. Under increasingly greater pressure from our customer, we were too often forced to do something which put us in a high-risk position, which eventually resulted in failure. Since last-minute change is a way of life, the lesson learned is that all our planning, systems, and capabilities have to be more flexible.

- The planning model was too complex: We had a cross-functional, cross-team group that put together a master model of the "right way" to execute a program. This model incorporated our WBS, including relationships, durations, responsibilities, etc. The final model incorporated over 600 separate tasks using Microsoft Project. The resulting model was simply too complex to serve as a value-added tool.

- Metrics work!: The QOS metric system provided a mechanism to focus and guide our activity.

Gregerson then commented on what he is currently doing at BTR to accelerate the process toward excellence:

- Training: Effective program management must focus on much more than simply the techniques to plan, execute, track, and control programs. Equally important to a program's success are the "softer" skill sets such as personal mastery, leadership, and team building. Leadership in particular is one of the most important, yet less trained, aspects of project management. As a starting point of evoking my new organization, I focused on training key associates using the best programs available anywhere in both the hard and soft skill sets.

- Direct global linkages: The revised solid-line matrix organization incorporated three basic changes versus my prior organization: (1) Centers of Excellence were directly matrixed with the Customer Focused Teams, (2) the COEs are directly aligned to our global organization, and (3) the CFTs are linked globally to ensure global customer focus, coordination, and support.

- Planning simplified value-added events: We left the complex models behind and instead focused on centralized planning of only significant events and key deliverables. We reduced those tracked by the program team from over 600 to about 30. This significantly improved the flexibility and user-friendliness of the model. We also increased the number of significant "value-added events" in the same line. These included senior management reviews (often named gateways), fresh eyes design reviews, design reviews, and process reviews. Detailed planning within the work breakdown structure is the responsibility of each function entity.

- Communication: No single element is more important than effective communication. All too often teams believe they do not have time for yet another meeting. We have implemented clockwork team meetings, where the team is brought together once a week (same day, same time, same location) via virtual co-location tools such as video conferencing and teleconferencing. The clockwork scheduling drastically improves the team ability to maintain a high level of participation.

When an organization is managed poorly, change is very slow and tedious. But when an organization is managed well, change can be swift. Consider the following sequence of events in the BTR Sealing Systems Group:

- January 1996: Gateway process was established.
- August 1996: The reorganization was accompanied by training and added discipline.
- August-December 1996: PMI certification was required for all project managers.
- November 1996: The program office was created.
- November 1996: The Global BTR Program Management Team was created.
- December 1996: The QOS metrics for program management and customer satisfaction were finalized.

Gregerson's goal is to create a well-focused team management system that improves with each new assignment. Gregerson believes that in the future the definition of excellence must also include the team:

> The missing element in the definition of excellence is the project team. A successful project must also be measured in how the team strengthened, learned, and enjoyed the project. This is … like exercising to get stronger to perform better—so must an organization.

Changing Times

Once the executives of a company recognize the need for flexibility, project management practice begins to evolve toward excellence. Table 13-1 summarizes the way most excellent companies view project management present and future. Today and tomorrow, project managers will need to know the business of their companies. Shared authority arrangements and nondedicated project teams will be the norm everywhere except in very large organizations that can afford dedicated teams.

Table 13-1. Changing times for project management.

Factor	Past View	Present View	Future View
Definition of success	Technical terms only	Time, cost, technology, and customer acceptance	Time, cost, technology, and customer acceptance; minimum scope changes; no business disturbance
Project manager's background	Technical	Technical or nontechnical	Must understand the business
Organization	Dedicated teams	Partially dedicated teams	Nondedicated teams
Authority	Project manager has maximum authority	Project and line managers share authority	Shared authority with team empowerment
Human resources	Negotiate for best people	Negotiate for best team	Negotiate for results
Team building	Sensitivity sessions	Selected coursework	Certification training and curriculum development

Many of these changes didn't happen by themselves. The evolution of the project management process was accelerated by the acceptance of concurrent engineering and total quality management. Table 13-2 shows the impact that concurrent engineering has had on project management. Project managers are now dedicated to one project to allow adequate risk management. To perform risk management, especially business risk management, the project managers must understand the business. Strong integration skills may become a necessity if business risks are to be mitigated.

Table 13-2. Concurrent engineering and change.

| CRITICAL ISSUES | PRESENT ORGANIZATION | | NEW ORGANIZATION |
	Project-Driven	Non-Project-Driven	Concurrent Engineering
Number of hats for the project manager	1	2	1
Availability	Full-time	Part-time	Full-time
Primary skill required	Understand technology, understand people	Technical expert, understand people	Knowledge of business, risk management, integration skills
Career path	Line manager to project manager to executive	Project manager to line manager to executive	Multiple
Promotion ladders	Management, technical, project management	Management, technical	Management, technical, project management
Project management department	Yes	No	Yes
Certification required in the near future	Probably	No	Highly probable

To add professionalism to the practice of project management, companies are creating project management departments. The departments sometimes provide an advantage over competitors in submitting bids. Project management departments usually expose the need for a triple-ladder career path: a management ladder, a technical ladder, and a project management ladder. The idea behind the project management ladder is quite simple. When a project manager becomes experienced in the project management ladder and enjoys the assignments given, why risk changing his or her job and/or ladder for advancement?

By combining Tables 13-1 and 13-2, we can create Table 13-3 to give us a glimpse into the evolving present and future state of excellent project management. Executive recognition of the need for flexibility has allowed corporations to restructure into strategic business units. The project managers within the strategic business units are more business managers than technical managers. The line managers who have the ultimate responsibility for the technical quality of the project or product now share accountability with the project manager.

Table 13-3. Project management's evolutionary process.

Time Frame	WBS Level at Which PM Executes	PM Educational Background	Organizational Structure	Accountability
early 1960s	Technical levels of WBS	Engineering	Traditional	With line managers
late 1960s	Technical levels of WBS	Mostly engineering, some business	Strong matrix	With PMs
1970s–1980s	Management levels of WBS	Mostly business, some engineering	Weak Matrix	Partially shared
1990s	Management levels of WBS	Mostly business, some engineering	SBU project management	Totally shared

The future of project management will be driven by both the customer and the contractor. Contractors who recognize the need for change will be the rising stars of the next century. The future will be team management on a global basis. The stars of tomorrow have already planned for this.

Linda Kretz, president and chief operating officer of 20/20 Solutions, predicts the project manager's role in the future:

Project management as a professional discipline is undergoing a metamorphosis. Corporations today no longer use the term "project management" to describe a variety of functions which can be characterized as expediting or brute force coordination. The difference between project management and these other functions lies mainly in the expectations of the client or sponsor and when the project manager is assigned to the project.

Project management in the future will be a multifaceted discipline which recognizes project managers for the value they bring to the corporate bottom line instead of a cost center perceived in the same way internal audits are viewed. Killing the messenger will be a thing of the past, because the message will meet the expectations of the stakeholders. Instead of finding out at the end of the fiscal year that corporate financial margins have not been met, project managers will have the capability to avert disaster by proactively managing the process rather than reacting to ongoing risks.

Project management will be viewed as a value-added entity. Project managers will be considered professionals, capable of enhancing the bottom line.... They will be the catalyst for corporate change. They will be viewed as having the ability to participate in economic justification for projects, in feasibility studies, and have the authority and empowerment to manage the project budget.

Emerging technology and project management will catapult businesses successfully into the twenty-first century. Those companies who prefer the status quo may find themselves without customers.

Suggested Readings

Carr, D. K., and Johansson, H. J. *Best Practices in Reengineering*. New York: McGraw-Hill, 1995.

Chapman, C., and Ward, S. *Project Risk Management*. New York: John Wiley and Sons, 1997.

Cleland, D. I. *Project Management: Strategic Design and Implementation*. New York: McGraw-Hill, 1994.

Cleland, D. I. *Field Guide to Project Management*. New York: Van Nostrand Reinhold, 1997.

Fitz-Enz, J. *The Eight Practices of Exceptional Companies*. New York: AMACOM Books, 1997.

Frame, J. D. *The New Project Management*. San Francisco: Jossey-Bass Publishers, 1994.

Galpin, T. J. *The Human Side of Change*. San Francisco: Jossey-Bass Publishers, 1996.

Kerzner, H. *Project Management: A Systems Approach to Planning, Scheduling, and Controlling*, 6th edition. New York: Van Nostrand Reinhold, 1997.

Kostner, J. *Virtual Leadership*. New York: Time-Warner Books, 1996.

Lindsay, W. M., and Petrick, J. A. *Total Quality and Organizational Development*. Del Ray Beach, FL: St. Lucie Press, 1996.

Lientz, B. P., and Ross, K. P. *Project Management for the 21st Century*. San Diego: Academic Press, 1995.

Pfeffer, J. *Competitive Advantage through People*. New York: McGraw-Hill, 1996.

Pinto, J. K. *Power & Politics in Project Management*. Upper Darby, PA: Project Management Institute, 1996.

Pont, T. *Investing in Training and Development*. East Brunswick, NJ: Nichols Publishing, 1996.

Toney, F., and Powers, R. *Best Practices of Project Management Groups in Large Functional Organizations.* Upper Darby. PA: Project Management Institute, 1997.

Trompenaars, F. *Riding the Waves of Culture.* Burr Ridge, IL: Irwin Professional Publishers, 1997.

Wellings, R. *Empowered Teams.* San Francisco: Jossey-Bass Publishers, 1993.

Project Management Maturity Questionnaire

On the next several pages you will find 20 questions concerning how mature you believe your organization to be. Beside each question you will circle the number that corresponds to your opinion. In the example below, the choice indicated is "Slightly Agree."

-3   Strongly Disagree

-2   Disagree

-1   Slightly Disagree

0   No Opinion

(+1)   Slightly Agree

+2   Agree

+3   Strongly Agree

Example: (-3, -2, -1, 0 (+1) +2, +3)

The row of numbers from -3 to +3 will be used later for evaluating the results. After answering Question No. 20, you will grade the exercise.

The following 20 questions involve **maturity**. Please answer each question as honestly as possible. Circle the answer you feel is correct, not the answer you think the instructor is looking for.

1. My company recognizes the **need** for project management. This **need** is recognized at all levels of management, including senior management.   -3 -2 -1 0 +1 +2 +3

2. My company has a system in place to manage both cost and schedule. The system requires charge numbers and cost account codes. The system **reports variances** from planned targets.   -3 -2 -1 0 +1 +2 +3

3. My company has recognized the **benefits** that are possible from implementing project management. These **benefits** have been recognized at all levels of management, including senior management.   -3 -2 -1 0 +1 +2 +3

4. My company (or division) has a
   well-defined project management
   methodology using life cycle phases.   - 3   - 2   - 1   0   + 1   + 2   + 3

5. Our executives visibly support project
   management through executive
   presentations, correspondence, and by
   occasionally attending project team
   meetings/briefings.   - 3   - 2   - 1   0   + 1   + 2   + 3

6. My company is committed to quality
   up-front planning. We try to do the best
   we can at planning.   - 3   - 2   - 1   0   + 1   + 2   + 3

7. Our lower and middle-level line
   managers totally and visibly support
   the project management process.   - 3   - 2   - 1   0   + 1   + 2   + 3

8. My company is doing everything
   possible to minimize "creeping"
   scope (i.e., scope changes) on our
   products.   - 3   - 2   - 1   0   + 1   + 2   + 3

9. Our line managers are committed
   not only to project management, but
   also to the promises made to project
   managers for deliverables.   - 3   - 2   - 1   0   + 1   + 2   + 3

10. The executives in my organization
    have a good understanding of the
    principles of project management.   - 3   - 2   - 1   0   + 1   + 2   + 3

11. My company has selected one or more
    project management software packages
    to be used as the project tracking
    system.   - 3   - 2   - 1   0   + 1   + 2   + 3

12. Our lower and middle-level line
    managers have been trained and
    educated in project management.   - 3   - 2   - 1   0   + 1   + 2   + 3

13. Our executives both understand
    project sponsorship and serve as
    project sponsors on selected projects.   - 3   - 2   - 1   0   + 1   + 2   + 3

14. Our executives have recognized or
    identified the **applications** of project
    management to various parts of our
    business.   - 3   - 2   - 1   0   + 1   + 2   + 3

15. My company has successfully **integrated** cost and schedule control together for both managing projects and reporting status.

- 3   - 2   - 1   0   + 1   + 2   + 3

16. My company has developed a project management curriculum (i.e., more than one or two courses) to enhance the project management skills of our employees.

- 3   - 2   - 1   0   + 1   + 2   + 3

17. Our executives have recognized what must be done in order to achieve maturity in project management.

- 3   - 2   - 1   0   + 1   + 2   + 3

18. My company views and treats project management as a profession rather than a part-time assignment.

- 3   - 2   - 1   0   + 1   + 2   + 3

19. Our lower- and middle-level line managers are willing to release their employees for project management training.

- 3   - 2   - 1   0   + 1   + 2   + 3

20. Our executives have demonstrated a willingness to change our way of doing business in order to mature in project management.

- 3   - 2   - 1   0   + 1   + 2   + 3

SCORING SHEET

Each response you circles in Questions 1–20 had a column value between -3 and +3. In the appropriate spaces below, place the circles value (between -3 and +3) beside each question.

Embryonic	Executive	Line Management	Growth	Maturity
#1_____	#5_____	#7_____	#4_____	#2_____
#3_____	#10_____	#9_____	#6_____	#15_____
#14_____	#13_____	#12_____	#8_____	#16_____
#17_____	#20_____	#19_____	#11_____	#18_____
Total_____	Total_____	Total_____	Total_____	Total_____

Transpose your total score in each category to the table below by placing an "X" in the appropriate area.

	Points											
	-12	-10	-8	-6	-4	-2	0	+2	+4	+6	+8	+10	+12

Stages

Maturity

Growth

Line
Management

Executive

Embryonic

Grading System

High scores (usually +6 or greater) indicate that these evolutionary stages of maturity have been achieved or at least you are now in this stage. Stages with very low numbers have not been achieved yet.

Consider the following scores:

Embryonic:	+8
Executive:	+10
Line Management:	+8
Growth:	+3
Maturity:	-4

This indicates that you have probably completed the first three stages and are now entering the Growth Stage. Keep in mind that the answers are not always this simple because companies can achieve portions of one stage in parallel with portions of a second or third stage.

Project Management
Excellence Questionnaire

On the next several pages are 42 multiple choice questions which will allow you to compare your organization against those companies that are discussed in this text. After you complete Question 42, a grading system is provided. You can then benchmark your organization against some of the best.

1. My company *actively* uses the following processes:

   A. Total quality management (TQM) only
   B. Concurrent engineering (shortening deliverable development time) only
   C. TQM and concurrent engineering only
   D. Risk management only
   E. Risk management and concurrent engineering only
   F. Risk management, concurrent engineering, and TQM

2. On what percent of your projects do you use the principles of total quality management?

   A. 0 percent
   B. 5–10 percent
   C. 11–25 percent
   D. 26–50 percent
   E. 51–75 percent
   F. 76–100 percent

3. On what percent of your projects do you use the principles of risk management?

   A. 0 percent
   B. 5–10 percent
   C. 11–25 percent
   D. 26–50 percent
   E. 51–75 percent
   F. 76–100 percent

4. On what percent of your projects do you try to compress product/deliverable schedules by performing work in parallel rather than in series?

   A. 0 percent
   B. 5–10 percent

     C. 11–25 percent
     D. 26–50 percent
     E. 51–75 percent
     F. 76–100 percent

5. My company's risk management process is based upon:

     A. We do not use risk management
     B. Financial risks only
     C. Technical risks only
     D. Scheduling risks only
     E. A combination of financial, technical, and scheduling risks based upon the project.

6. The risk management methodology in my company is:

     A. Nonexistent
     B. More informal rather than formal
     C. Based upon a structured methodology supported by policies and procedures
     D. Based upon a structured methodology supported by policies, procedures, and standardized forms to be completed

7. How many different project management methodologies exist in your organization? (Note: Consider a systems development methodology for MIS projects different than a product development project management methodology.)

     A. We have no methodologies.
     B. 1
     C. 2–3
     D. 4–5
     E. More than 5

8. With regard to benchmarking,

     A. My company has never tried to use benchmarking.
     B. My company has performed benchmarking and implemented changes but not for project management.
     C. My company has performed project management benchmarking but no changes were made.
     D. My company has performed project management benchmarking and changes were made.

9. Which of the following best describes your corporate culture:

     A. Single boss reporting
     B. Multiple boss reporting
     C. Dedicated teams without empowerment

    D.   Nondedicated teams without empowerment

    E.   Dedicated teams with empowerment

    F.   Nondedicated team with empowerment

10. With regard to morals and ethics, my company believes that:

    A.   The customer is always right

    B.   Decision be made in the following sequence: best interest of the customer first, then the company, then the employees.

    C.   Decisions *should* be made in the following sequence: best interest of company first, customer second, and the employees last.

    D.   We have no such written policy or set of standards.

11. My company conducts internal training courses on:

    A.   Morality and ethics within the company

    B.   Morality and ethics in dealing with customers

    C.   Good business practices

    D.   All of the above

    E.   None of the above

    F.   At least two of the first three

12. With regard to scope creep or scope changes, our culture:

    A.   Discourages changes after project initiation

    B.   Allows changes only up to a certain point in the project's life cycle using a formal change control process

    C.   Allows changes anywhere in the project life cycle using a formal change control process

    D.   Allows changes but without any formal control process

13. Our culture seems to be based upon:

    A.   Policies

    B.   Procedures (including forms to be filled out)

    C.   Policies and procedures

    D.   Guidelines

    E.   Policies, procedures, and guidelines

14. Cultures are either quantitative (policies, procedures, forms, and guidelines), behavioral, or a compromise. The culture in my company is probably _____ percent behavioral.

    A.   10–25

    B.   26–50

    C.   51–60

    D.   61–75

    E.   Greater than 75

15. Our organizational structure is:

    A. Traditional (predominantly vertical)
    B. A strong matrix (i.e., project manager provides most of the technical direction)
    C. A weak matrix (i.e., line managers provide most of the technical direction)
    D. We use co-located teams
    E. I don't know what the structure is. Management changes it on a daily basis.

16. When assigned as a project leader, our project manager obtains resources by:

    A. "Fighting" for the best people available
    B. Negotiating with line managers for the best people available
    C. Negotiating for deliverables rather than people
    D. Using senior management to help get the appropriate people
    E. Taking whatever we get, no questions asked

17. Our line managers:

    A. Accept total accountability for the work in their line
    B. Ask the project managers to accept total accountability
    C. Try to share accountability with the project managers
    D. Hold the assigned employees accountable
    E. We don't know the meaning of the work "accountability." It is not part of our vocabulary.

18. In the culture within our company, the person most likely held accountable for the ultimate technical integrity of the final deliverable is/are:

    A. The assigned employees
    B. The project manager
    C. The line manager
    D. The project sponsor
    E. The whole team

19. In our company, the project manager's authority comes from:

    A. Within himself/herself, whatever they can get away with
    B. The immediate superior to the project manager
    C. Documented job description
    D. Informally through the project sponsor in the form of a project charter or appointment letter

20. After project go-ahead, our project sponsors tend to:

    A. Become invisible, even when needed
    B. Micromanage

C. Expect summary-level briefings once a week
D. Expect summary-level briefings once every two weeks
E. Get involved only when a critical problem occurs or at the request of the project manager or line managers.

21. What percentage of your projects have sponsors who are at the director level or above?

A. 0–10 percent
B. 11–25 percent
C. 26–50 percent
D. 51–75 percent
E. More than 75 percent

22. My company offers approximately how many different *internal* training courses for the employees? (Courses that can be regarded as project related)

A. Less than 5
B. 6–10
C. 11–20
D. 21–30
E. More than 30

23. With regard to your previous answer, what percentage of the courses are more behavioral than quantitative?

A. Less than 10 percent
B. 10–25 percent
C. 26–50 percent
D. 51–75 percent
E. More than 75 percent

24. My company believes that:

A. Project management is a part-time job
B. Project management is a profession
C. Project management is a profession and we should become certified as project management professionals but at our own expense
D. Project management is a profession and our company pays for us to become certified as project management professionals
E. We have no project managers in our company

25. My company believes that training should be:

A. Performed at the request of employees
B. Performed to satisfy a short-term need
C. Performed to satisfy both long and short-term needs

D.　Should be performed only if these exists a return on investment on training dollars

26.　My company believes that the content of training courses is best determined by the:

A.　Instructor
B.　Human resource department
C.　Management
D.　Employees who will receive the training
E.　Customization after an audit of the employees and managers

27.　What percentage of the training courses in project management contain *documented* lessons-learned case studies from other projects within your company?

A.　None
B.　Less than 10 percent
C.　11–25 percent
D.　26–50 percent
E.　More than 50 percent

28.　What percentage of the executives in your functional (not corporate) organization have attended training programs or executive briefings specifically designed to show executives what they can do to help project management mature?

A.　None! Our executives know everything
B.　Less than 25 percent
C.　26–50 percent
D.　51–75 percent
E.　More than 75 percent

29.　In my company, employees are promoted to management because:

A.　They are technical experts
B.　They demonstrate the administrative skills of a professional manager
C.　They know how to make sound business decisions
D.　They are at the top of their pay grade
E.　We have no place else to put them

30.　A report must be written and presented to the customer. Neglecting the cost to accumulate the information, the approximate cost per page for a typical report is:

A.　I have no idea
B.　$100–200 per page
C.　$201–500 per page
D.　Greater than $500 per page
E.　Free; exempt employees in our company prepare the reports at home on their own time

31. Which of the following best describes the culture within your organization?

   A. Informal project management based upon trust, communication, and cooperation
   B. Formality based upon policies and procedures for everything
   C. Project management thrives on formal authority relationships
   D. Executive meddling which forces an overabundance of documentation
   E. Nobody trusts the decisions of our project managers

32. What percentage of the project manager's time each week is spent preparing reports?

   A. 5-10 percent
   B 11-20 percent
   C. 21-40 percent
   D. 41-60 percent
   E. Greater than 60 percent

33. During project *planning,* most of our activities are accomplished using:

   A. Policies
   B. Procedures
   C. Guidelines
   D. Checklists
   E. None of the above

34. The typical time duration for a project status review meeting with senior management is:

   A. Less than 30 minutes
   B. 30-60 minutes
   C. 61-90 minutes
   D. 91 minutes-2 hours
   E. Greater than 2 hours

35. Our customers mandate that we manage our projects:

   A. Informally
   B. Formally, but without customer meddling
   C. Formally, but with customer meddling
   D. It is our choice as long as the deliverables are met

36. My company believes that *poor* employees:

   A. Should never be assigned to teams
   B. Once assigned to a team, are the responsibility of the project manager for supervision

C. Once assigned to a team, are the responsibility of the line manager for supervision
D. Can be effective if assigned to the right team
E. Should be promoted into management

37. Employees who are assigned to a project team (either full-time or part-time) have a performance evaluation conducted by:

A. Their line manager only
B. The project manager only
C. Both the project and line managers
D. Both the project and line managers, together with a review by the sponsor

38. Which pair of skills will probably be the most important for project managers of your company in the twenty-first century?

A. Technical knowledge and leadership
B. Risk management and knowledge of the business
C. Integration skills and risk management
D. Integration skills and knowledge of the business
E. Communication skills and technical understanding

39. In my organization, the people assigned as project leaders are usually:

A. First-line managers
B. First- or second-line managers
C. Any level of management
D. Usually nonmanagement employees
E. Anyone in the company

40. The project managers in my organization have undergone at least some degree of training in:

A. Feasibility studies
B. Cost-benefit analyses
C. Both A and B
D. Our project managers are brought on board after project approval/award.

41. Our project managers are encouraged to:

A. Take risks
B. Take risks upon approval by senior management
C. Take risks upon approval of project sponsors
D. Avoid risks

42. Consider the following statement: Our project managers have a sincere interest in what happens to each team member *after* the project is scheduled to be completed.

   A.   Strongly agree
   B.   Agree
   C.   Not sure
   D.   Disagree
   E.   Strongly disagree

The assignment of the points is as follows:

INTEGRATED PROCESSES						
Questions			**Points**			
1.	A. 2	B. 2	C. 4	D. 2	E. 4	F. 5
2.	A. 0	B. 0	C. 1	D. 3	E. 4	F. 5
3.	A. 0	B. 0	C. 3	D. 4	E. 5	F. 5
4.	A. 0	B. 1	C. 3	D. 4	E. 5	F. 5
5.	A. 0	B. 2	C. 2	D. 2	E. 5	
6.	A. 0	B. 2	C. 4	D. 5		
7.	A. 0	B. 5	C. 4	D. 2	E. 0	

CULTURE						
Questions	**Points**					
8.	A. 0	B. 2	C. 3	D. 5		
9.	A. 1	B. 3	C. 4	D. 4	E. 5	F. 5
10.	A. 1	B. 5	C. 4	D. 0		
11.	A. 3	B. 3	C. 3	D. 5	E. 0	F. 4
12.	A. 1	B. 5	C. 5	D. 3		
13.	A. 2	B. 3	C. 4	D. 5	E. 4	
14.	A. 2	B. 3	C. 4	D. 5	E. 5	

MANAGEMENT SUPPORT					
Questions			**Points**		
15.	A. 1	B. 5	C. 5	D. 5	E. 0
16.	A. 2	B. 3	C. 5	D. 0	E. 2
17.	A. 4	B. 2	C. 5	D. 1	E. 0
18.	A. 2	B. 3	C. 5	D. 0	E. 3
19.	A. 1	B. 2	C. 2	D. 4	E. 5
20.	A. 1	B. 1	C. 3	D. 4	E. 5
21.	A. 1	B. 3	C. 5	D. 4	E. 4

TRAINING AND EDUCATION					
Questions			**Points**		
22.	A. 1	B. 3	C. 5	D. 5	E. 5
23.	A. 0	B. 2	C. 4	D. 5	E. 5
24.	A. 0	B. 3	C. 4	D. 5	E. 0
25.	A. 2	B. 3	C. 4	D. 5	
26.	A. 2	B. 1	C. 2	D. 3	E. 5
27.	A. 0	B. 1	C. 3	D. 5	E. 5
28.	A. 0	B. 1	C. 3	D. 4	E. 5

INFORMAL PROJECT MANAGEMENT					
Questions			**Points**		
29.	A. 2	B. 4	C. 5	D. 1	E. 0
30.	A. 0	B. 3	C. 4	D. 5	E. 0
31.	A. 5	B. 2	C. 3	D. 1	E. 0
32.	A. 3	B. 5	C. 4	D. 2	E. 1
33.	A. 2	B. 3	C. 4	D. 5	E. 0
34.	A. 4	B. 5	C. 3	D. 1	E. 0
35.	A. 3	B. 4	C. 3	D. 5	

BEHAVIORAL EXCELLENCE					

Questions			Points		
36.	A. 1	B. 2	C. 4	D. 5	E. 0
37.	A. 3	B. 1	C. 5	D. 2	E. 0
38.	A. 3	B. 5	C. 5	D. 5	E. 4
39.	A. 2	B. 2	C. 2	D. 5	E. 3
40.	A. 3	B. 3	C. 5	D. 1	
41.	A. 5	B. 3	C. 4	D. 1	
42.	A. 5	B. 4	C. 2	D. 1	E. 1

Determine your points for each of the questions and complete the following:

A. Points for integrated Processes (Questions 1-7):   _____

B. Points for Culture (Questions 8-14):   _____

C. Points for Management Support (Questions 15-21):   _____

D. Points for Training and Education (Questions 22-28):   _____

E. Points for Informal Project Management (Questions 29-35):   _____

F. Points for Behavioral Excellence (Questions 36-42):   _____

                                        Total: _____

Each of the six areas are components of the Hexagon of Excellence discussed in Chapter 6. The total points can be interpreted as follows:

Points	Interpretation
168–210	Your company compares very well to the companies discussed in this text. You are on the right track for excellence, assuming that you have not achieved it yet. Continuous improvement will occur.
147–168	Your company is going in the right direction, but more work is still needed. Project management is not totally perceived as a profession. It is also possible that your organization simply does not fully understand project management. Emphasis is probably more toward being nonproject-driven than project-driven.

Points	Interpretation
80–146	The company is probably just providing lip service to project management. Support is minimal. The company believes that it is the right thing to do, but has not figured out the true benefits or what they, the executives, should be doing. The company is still a functional organization.
79 and Below	Perhaps you should change jobs or seek another profession. The company has no understanding of project management, nor does it appear that the company wishes to change. Line managers want to maintain their existing power base and may feel threatened by project management.

Indexes

Subject